KU-711-721

CHICAGO
ENCOUNTER

NATE CAVALIERI

Chicago Encounter

Published by Lonely Planet Publications Pty Ltd
ABN 36 005 607 983

Australia	Head Office, Locked Bag 1, Footscray, Vic 3011
	☎ 03 8379 8000 fax 03 8379 8111
	talk2us@lonelyplanet.com.au
USA	150 Linden St, Oakland, CA 94607
	☎ 510 250 6400
	toll free 800 275 8555
	fax 510 893 8572
	info@lonelyplanet.com
UK	2nd fl, 186 City Rd
	London EC1V 2NT
	☎ 020 7106 2100 fax 020 7106 2101
	go@lonelyplanet.co.uk

This title was commissioned in Lonely Planet's Oakland office and produced by: **Commissioning Editor** Jennye Garibaldi **Coordinating Editors** Michelle Bennett, Charlotte Orr **Coordinating Cartographers** Xavier Di Toro, Corey Hutchinson **Layout Designer** Nicholas Colicchia **Senior Editors** Helen Christinis, Katie Lynch **Managing Cartographer** Adrian Persoglia **Cover Designer** Katy Murenu **Project Manager** Rachel Imeson **Managing Layout Designers** Sally Darmody, Laura Jane Thanks to Sasha Baskett, Jessica Boland, Carol Jackson, Alison Lyall, Erin Richards

ISBN 978 1 74179 292 8

Printed through Colorcraft Ltd, Hong Kong.
Printed in China.

Acknowledgement CTA Map © 2009 Chicago Transit Authority.

HOW TO USE THIS BOOK
Colour-Coding & Maps

Colour-coding is used for symbols on maps and in the text that they relate to (eg all eating venues on the maps and in the text are given a green knife and fork symbol). Each neighborhood also gets its own colour, and this is used down the edge of the page and throughout that neighborhood section.

Shaded yellow areas on the maps denote 'areas of interest' – for their historical significance, their attractive architecture or their great bars and restaurants. We encourage you to head to these areas and just start exploring!

Send us your feedback We love to hear from readers – your comments help make our books better. We read every word you send us, and we always guarantee that your feedback goes straight to the appropriate authors. The most useful submissions are rewarded with a free book. To send us your updates and find out about Lonely Planet events, newsletters and travel news, visit our award-winning website: *lonelyplanet.com/contact*.

Note: We may edit, reproduce and incorporate your comments in Lonely Planet products such as guidebooks, websites and digital products, so let us know if you don't want your comments reproduced or your name acknowledged. For a copy of our privacy policy visit *lonelyplanet.com/privacy*.

NATE CAVALIERI

As a kid, Nate remembers taking an elevator to the top of the 'City of Big Shoulders' at dusk, peering out at the landscape of twinkling headlights, steaming factories and snow-covered lots thinking '*This* is a city.' Some 20 years later, standing in front of 'The Bean' or the Hideout bar painted with a three-story mural of Barack Obama, that feeling of awe has only grown. A native of northern Michigan, Nate studied music and creative writing at Oberlin College, spent a few derelict years playing piano and organ in Chicago's clubs and lived in Chicago while researching Lonely Planet's 5th edition of *Chicago*. He is also the coauthor of Lonely Planet guides to Puerto Rico and California, and *Volunteer: A Travelers Guide To Making A Difference Around the World*.

NATE'S THANKS

Nate's been lucky to work under the good-spirited guidance of Jennye Garibaldi, who he taunted with emails about country fried bacon. Alison Lyall and Sasha Baskett have been immensely helpful with technical aspects of the book, and Charlotte Orr made careful edits.

Thanks to friends who made research a delight: Jesse, Ben, Katrin, James and Charlie. In addition to thanks, he owes Maria Krasinski a piece of French cookware and Rob Wildeboer a new bike.

THE PHOTOGRAPHER

Charles Cook has been a freelance photographer for 17 years and is based in the Chicago area. His first few years in the industry were spent working in commercial studios in Chicago. Since then he has concentrated on travel photography and has been contributing to Lonely Planet Images for nine years, with images published in several Lonely Planet guidebooks. Other clients include the American Automobile Association (AAA), *Backpacker* magazine, The Nature Conservancy, *Sierra* magazine and numerous others.

Leave your blues behind at this Chicago History Museum (p69) exhibit, Old Town

CONTENTS

THIS IS CHICAGO

'If there is anyone out there who still doubts that America is a place where all things are possible,' begins Barack Obama, '…tonight is your answer.' But in the frosty, electric air above Grant Park we're not just anywhere in America: we're in Chicago.

After the tens of thousands hear their junior senator, a former community organizer in Chicago's checkered South Side, accept the highest political office, many walk in a daze up Michigan Ave under the towering night-lit monuments of the city in which they live, crying and laughing, elated and overwhelmed.

Of course, no story of Chicago goes without being dichotomous opposites, and even as the afterglow of that evening faded, another brutal winter brought headlines of political scandal and economic asperity.

But all the way down the line, the essence of Chicago has duplicity unlike any other American city – a place where high- and lowbrow art makes a messy collision, where restaurants are equally notable for cutting-edge concepts like molecular gastronomy and burly bricks of sausage-stuffed deep-dish. Residents in the 'city that works' play pretty damn hard too – sprawling on sandy beaches, packing bars until 5am and whiling away an entire summer with outdoor festivals.

But when you approach the heart of the city from one of the highways that connect it to the rest of the pancake-flat Midwest and its airports, the cluster of buildings that rises so dramatically above the glassy surface of Lake Michigan might well make you gasp. The clattering roar of the El train passing overhead announces that Chicago is seizing its moment in history. A place where all things are possible: *this* is Chicago.

Top left Intimate indie rock venue Schubas (p91), Lake View **Top right** Frank Gehry's brilliant, metallic Jay Pritzker Pavilion (p10), Millennium Park **Bottom** Read all about Chicago's latest hero at 57th Street Books (p144), Hyde Park

\>HIGHLIGHTS

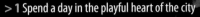

Twinkling architectural beauties form a guard of honor along the majestic Chicago River, Downtown

>1 MILLENNIUM PARK
SPEND A DAY IN THE PLAYFUL HEART OF THE CITY

The colossal head of a crazy-looking old lady – four stories high! – is spewing a gush of water onto a gaggle of squealing children. In the distance, the spires of the city rise into the clear blue air, along which floats a faint orchestral strain. Sure, you could get on the El and spend the day racing around the city by foot, but you'd probably learn just as much about the character of the city by spending a long, lazy afternoon soaking in the city's centerpiece, Millennium Park.

To consider this as merely a public park would be dialing your expectations *way* too low. The most exciting public space in the United States? Now that's a bit more accurate. Yet, somehow, it's even more than that – snuggled between the stone and metal forest of the Loop and sweeping shores of Lake Michigan, the park is Chicago's beating heart, the calling card of the city, a place that offers a sampling menu of the big adventures ahead.

If you approach Millennium Park from the west, its sun-drenched sculptures stand in dazzling contrast to the shadowed corridors of the Loop. The first thing to catch your eye will be Frank Gehry's 120ft tall band shell, the Jay Pritzker Pavilion, shining like the city's brilliant metallic crown. Throughout the summer, recline on the grass to check out a rehearsal of the Grant Park Orchestra or a concert calendar that ranges from Afrobeat to indie rock. If you arrive from the south, you'll get misted by Jaume Plensa's whimsical 50ft-high *Crown Fountain* (Map pp38–9), which projects video images of Chicagoans spitting out water onto squealing children throughout the summer. In winter the faces overlook the McCormick Tribune Ice Rink (p47), where locals glide along to a soundtrack of city music makers such as Wilco and Willie Dixon. The space also offers free dance lessons from Dance Chicago (p45). On the park's east side, the Gehry-designed BP bridge (Map pp38–9, F3) spans Columbus Dr and rewards those who stroll over it with great skyline views.

But regardless of when you come or how you get here, the thing that has become the park's biggest draw is 'The Bean' – officially *Cloud Gate* (Map pp38–9; pictured opposite) – Anish Kapoor's

brilliantly polished 110-ton silver sculpture, constantly abuzz with admirers. Stand in front of its bizarre, unearthly reflection and you'll take home a photo of a place that's different from most places you'll ever be – a vision of the world that's kind of like the one back home, but more playful and a bit warped and, above all, surprisingly beautiful. If it's the first photo you take on your visit to Chicago, it will be the first of many you might describe the same way.

See p41 for more information.

>2 CHICAGO BLUES

PLUG IN AND HEAR THE WINDY CITY WAIL

Whether it was the ghostly howl of blues forefather Robert Johnson or the bawdy wail of the genre's prodigal sons, The Blues Brothers, chances are the rolling, soul-stirred melody probably popped into your head on the way here: 'Oh baby don't you wanna go, back to that same old place, sweet home Chicago?' Chicago may have launched a huge number of musical movements, but none are as iconoclastic as the blues – a rude, raunchy, radically inspired take on the genre that's defined by screaming guitars, rolling bass lines and R&B-inflected rhythms. Today, modern blues makers have adopted a funkier gait and more cocksure vocals than their predecessors, but no visit to the city would be near complete without seeking out a blues hall and getting the blues in person. Buddy Guy's Legends (p138; pictured above) is one of the best, where a spacious floor plan, upscale soul cookin' and the dynamic presence of the namesake's owner give the place a legendary feel. If you want to experience something a bit more down and dirty, head to the South Side, where a couple of clubs – Rosa's Lounge (p119) and the New Checkerboard Lounge (p145) – might be short on frills but tall on authenticity. If you don't have time to see it in the flesh, pick up a platter of local blues at the Jazz Record Mart (p53).

>3 DEEP-DISH

HEFT A GOOEY SLICE OF THE CITY'S INFAMOUS AMBASSADORIAL DISH

You almost have to feel a little bad for the first pizzas in Chicago – a scrawny, sickly disk of baked dough that was hardly fit to carry the locally packed pork sausage that burdened its surface. But in the early 1940s Chicago's famed take on the dish – a true pizza *pie* – fell from the heavens with a thud. These behemoths are little like the pathetic comfort food known by the same name in the rest of the world; they're created in a special pan – kind of like a frying pan without the handle – so the dough, which encases a molten bed of mozzarella, tomato sauce and a heart-stopping collection of meats, can be oven fried. More than a few slices and you'll have to be rolled out.

The flagship Pizzeria Uno (p55) claims to have invented this bad mother, but, like any other pizza-related discussion in Chicago, this claim is a fertile topic for debate with the locals. Many flock to the brick Victorian that houses Pizzeria Uno for a taste, but the ubiquitous Giordano's (p55; pictured above) franchise offers beautifully made pies without the wait. Our favorite? A no-frills neighborhood joint called Pequod's Pizza (p74), where you get a gooey slice with a caramelized crust, without the tour bus crowds.

>4 ART INSTITUTE OF CHICAGO

STROLL AMONG IMPRESSIONISTS, ARMOR AND AMERICAN MASTERPIECES

You've passed the big bronze lions and entered one of the premiere art museums in the modern world: endless marble and glass corridors, room after room after room filled with paintings, textiles, sculpture and photographs – some quarter million in total – all of which demands ponderous chin-stroking hours of appreciation. So how do you start? Simple: lace up some comfortable sneakers and make a plan. There are Japanese prints, Grecian urns and 20th-century textiles, so grab a map at the desk and head for your favorite period, making sure to at least glance through the new Modern Wing. If you're more interested in an overview, take the free 'Highlights of the Art Institute' tour (2pm Tuesday, Saturday and Sunday). But, since you're standing in one of America's finest museums, even if you wander aimlessly, you're sure to bump into something awe-inspiring.

A visit here requires taking in the venerated collection of impressionist works, for which the museum is most widely known (seen *Ferris Bueller's Day Off* lately?). Just up the Grand Staircase into Room 201, Gustave Caillebotte's *Paris Street and Rainy Day* and Seurat's pointillist 1884 masterpiece *A Sunday Afternoon on La Grande Jatte* introduce this collection with appropriately muted fireworks. Through a doorway is Van Gogh's *The Bedroom*, painted during a stay at an asylum, and Monet's *Stack of Wheat*, part of a series that launched the artist's career in 1891.

UNEXPECTED GEMS OF THE ART INSTITUTE

> Great Hall of Arms and Armor – Enough of the paintings already! Let's joust!
> Thorne Miniature Rooms – These miniatures span 500 years of interiors, all as delicate as they are beautiful.
> Paperweight Collection – I know what you're thinking: 'Paperweights? I'm here for art!' But this collection of 1400 ornate desk accessories will amaze.
> North McCormick Courtyard – Rewards include fresh air and Alexander Calder's *Flying Dragon*, a little buddy to his similarly vivid *Flamingo* in the Loop.

The rest of the main building's treasures, depicting similar tales of madness and artistic triumph, can occupy the afternoon, from Picasso's *The Old Guitarist* to Salvador Dalí's nightmarish *Inventions of the Monsters*. Grant Wood's 1930 *American Gothic* – which pictures Wood's sister and dentist modeling as two austere farmers – and Edward Hopper's *Nighthawks* are here as well. Remember: comfortable sneakers.

Even though the perennial favorites will continue to draw armchair appreciators looking to see the source material from their calendars, the buzz at the institute these days is about the newly opened Modern Wing, a stark and stunning design by Pritzker Prize–winning architect Renzo Piano. The Modern Wing provides a new home for the museum's collection of 20th- and 21st-century art. The brilliant windows open up on Millennium Park at the city skyline, itself a masterpiece.

See p37 for more information.

>5 WRIGLEY FIELD

TAKE ME OUT TO THE BALLGAME...AND CONCILIATORY BEERS AFTERWARD

Set to a soundtrack of hollering sports junkies and high-fiving beer drinkers, a visit to Wrigleyville is a boisterous Chicago experience that's completely off the hook if the Cubs are at home. Built in 1914 and named for the chewing-gum magnate, Wrigley Field – aka 'The Friendly Confines' – is the second-oldest park in the major leagues, where a tangible sense of the ivy-covered history comes alive with legendary curses, playful traditions and a team that suffers some of the worst luck in US sports history.

But no matter that the hapless Cubbies haven't won a championship since 1908, shoveling down hot dogs with the riotous 'Bleacher Bums' makes for an unforgettable afternoon. It takes long foresight to get tickets, but if you don't, peep through the 'knothole,' a garage-door-sized opening on Sheffield Ave, to watch a bit of the game for free. Baseball junkies can take a 90-minute **tour** (☎ 773-404-2827; tours $25) on selected weekends of away games.

Even when there's no action on the field, there's plenty of gamesmanship in the bars and restaurants lining Clark St and Southport Ave. The neighborhood is a magnet for cruising singles and shoppers who are well mannered by day and keyed up after dark. When the Cubs *are* at home, look out: 40,000 fans descend on the 'hood, and party hard, win or lose.

See p79 for more information.

>6 LINCOLN PARK ZOO

CONVENE WITH SILVERBACKS AND ROACHES AT THE CITY'S BEST FREEBIE

Situated in the heart of the park and bordered by Lake Michigan, Lincoln Park's 'zoological garden' positions the oldest animal park in the US among rolling brick pathways and a jubilant display of flowers, making it one of Chicago's great remaining freebies (if you manage to forgive the $12 parking). Following the color-coded paths, visitors can get face time with slithery, cuddly and exotic animals from around the world. The elephants and other large leaf-chomping monsters make the Regenstein African Journey a favorite, and the Center For African Apes separates visitors from huge silverbacks by only a few inches of glass. For the kids the zoo's appeal is abundant: they'll squeal at the hissing cockroaches from Madagascar, and get their hands on the udder of a heifer at the Farm-in-the-Zoo.

See p69 for more information.

>7 CHICAGO ARCHITECTURE FOUNDATION RIVER CRUISE

FLOAT IN THE SHADOW OF CONCRETE AND STEEL GIANTS

Sure, it's possible to plunge into the concrete calamity of the Loop feet first, dodging crowds and cabs to stare at Chicago's magnificent buildings from the sidewalk. But the skyline takes on a surreal majesty as you float through its shadows on the Chicago River, and a river tour run by the Chicago Architecture Foundation (p42) is the best way to appreciate the finest collection of buildings in the United States.

Though tragic human and natural disasters have laid waste to a number of American cities over the nation's history, none has rebounded quite as powerfully as Chicago did in the years after the Chicago Fire in 1871. After the blaze made the city a blank canvas, Chicago became the center of American architectural innovation, drawing young, ambitious architects to rebuild and redesign the booming city. Dankmar Adler, Daniel Burnham, John Root and Louis Sullivan formed the 'Chicago School' (1872–99) to reinvent the skyline with steel framing and high-speed elevators, and a later movement, the so-called 'Prairie School' (1895–1915), delivered the nation's great architectural mind, Frank Lloyd Wright.

CHICAGO BUILDINGS THAT CHANGED THE WORLD

> Monadnock Building (Map pp38–9, D5) – the internal steel frame birthed the skyscraper.
> Reliance Building (Map pp38–9, D3) – the first skyscraper covered with plate-glass windows.
> Marina City (Map pp50–1, C5) – these giant corn cobs were conceived by Bertrand Goldberg as a 'city within a city.'
> Chicago Federal Center (Map pp38–9, D4) – Ludwig Mies van der Rohe's contemporary masterstroke.
> John Hancock Center (Map pp60–1) – an early example of a tubular system still used in the world's tallest buildings.
> Chicago Spire (p52) – Chicago's newest triumph will be the tallest building in America.

But even if you don't know your Prairie School from your *Prairie Home Companion,* the 90-minute river cruise is the best way to spend your time and money to get acquainted with the city. It offers a unique perspective on the two essential features that make Chicago so stunning – bold buildings and sparkling water. The guides are sharp-witted and knowledgeable, and as you float along they explain the birthplace of the modern skyscraper, and point out waterfront buildings that demonstrate the perfection of the form, including the gleaming Wrigley Building (Map pp50–1, D4) and the Sears Tower (p41).

If your crippling thalassophobia won't allow you to set foot on a boat, don't wander around in clueless awe of these giants on your own; look into taking one of the many excellent guided tours run by the Chicago Transit Authority (CTA). The two docent-led tours on the city's historic and modern skyscrapers ($12, two hours) are both excellent, and those who enjoy a bit of tipple with their touring can sign up for a happy-hour tour, which offers a series of regular trips and ends with a drink at a Loop restaurant (adult/senior or student $16/12; weekdays 5:30pm).

HIGHLIGHTS

>8 SECOND CITY
LAUGH TILL YOU CAN'T BREATHE AT BRILLIANTLY IMPROVISED COMEDY

A dead ringer for a disgraced local politico is at center stage, singing a '70s rock opera in a tracksuit. A woman contemplates becoming Facebook friends with a plate of runny eggs. A man rolls out on stage with a Superman cape tied around the back of his wheelchair.

These are but some of the biting, wickedly funny moments parading across Chicago's improv comedy stages nightly, scenarios invented moments after a booze-fueled suggestion is hollered from the darkened hall. Were it not for Chicago's Second City troupe, which began performing intentionally unstructured skits as the Compass Players in a Hyde Park bar in 1955, the proverbial chicken might still be crossing the road of American comedy. Audience participation was a key element, and the Second City (p77; pictured) theater made Chicago comedy synonymous with spontaneous, often fairly raunchy laughs.

Since it's one of Chicago's signature nightlife experiences, seeing improvised comedy at Second City is a way to pass an evening laughing your ass off. Before you roll in with your hilarious suggestion though, know that Second City stages a large variety of productions – some of which are nearly serious. If the offerings at Second City and its sundry training stage are unappealing or too expensive, there are other places to catch improv all over town, including IO (p90) and ComedySportz (p90).

>CHICAGO CALENDAR

Since Chicago isn't much for irony, its residents take their official motto 'City In a Garden' literally in the summer, relaxing in leafy tavern courtyards and sidewalk cafés, filling parks on balmy evenings for open-air concerts and hitting the streets on blazing afternoons for barbecue-scented festivals. When winter gales blow, the festival scene mostly hibernates, and shoppers strolling down slush-lined boulevards duck into corner taverns to warm up behind the steamy windows. For the city's official festival schedule, visit www.explorechicago.org or the excellent guide to nightlife and events at www.centerstagechicago.com.

The North Michigan Ave bridge ushering people into the city's heart

CHICAGO CALENDAR

JANUARY

New Year's Eve Fireworks at Buckingham Fountain
☎ 312-774-3370
The city sets off a huge arsenal of aerial explosives at Chicago's family fountain – an excellent (if chilly) way to bring in the New Year.

Polar Adventure Days
☎ 312-742-7529; www.chicagopark district.com
On select weekends throughout the winter, the Chicago Parks District hosts frigid family events on Northerly Island with sled dogs, ice sculptures and snowshoe-ing. Mush!

FEBRUARY

Black History Month
☎ 877-244-2246
Chicago hosts citywide events and exhibits to celebrate African American history, culminating with the birthday of Martin Luther King Jr.

Chinese New Year
www.chicagochinatown.org
Leaping dragons, sputtering firecrackers and greetings of 'Gung hay fat choy!' fill Wentworth Ave at this time of year; the exact date of Chinese New Year depends on an ancient calendar.

MARCH

Hellenic Heritage Greek Parade
☎ 773-775-4949; www.chicagogreek parade.com
Hellenic sons and daughters wave the blue-and-white flag for this late-March /early-April parade, which takes over Halsted St through the center of Greektown with gusto.

St Patrick's Day Parade
☎ 312-942-9188; www.chicagost patsparade.com
This colossal downtown parade ends with the local plumbers' union dying the Chicago River green. Seriously.

South Side Irish St Patrick's Day Parade
☎ 773-393-8687; www.southside irishparade.org
The city's proud 'Sout' Side Irish host the *other* St Patty's parade, complete with droning bagpipes and beer-addled boisterousness.

APRIL

Art Chicago
☎ 312-587-3300; www.artchicago.com
Thousands of artists fill the Merchandise Mart for Chicago's renowned international modern-art exhibition.

Young drummers getting into the festive spirit

Chicago Improv Festival
☎ 773-935-9810; www.chicago
improvfestival.org
The town that invented improv comedy
happily hosts its preeminent festival in
April, spitballing yucks throughout the
Windy City.

Green Apple Festival
www.greenapplefestival.com
This carbon-neutral Earth Day event features
citywide performances and kid's events at
the Lincoln Park Zoo.

MAY

Bike the Drive
www.bikethedrive.org
Cruising a carless Lakeshore Dr is worth the
sunrise start, hosted annually on the Sunday
before Memorial Day.

Cinco De Mayo Festival & Parade
☎ 773-843-9738
Pilsen, the center of Chicago's Mexican
community, and Douglas Park go on a
five-day bender with Mexican eats, floats
and music.

Great Chicago Places & Spaces
Festival
www.greatchicagoplaces.us
Hundreds of events, activities, and architectural and design tours, many of them
free, inspire awe (and craned necks) in the
birthplace of the skyscraper.

JUNE

Chicago Blues Festival

☎ 312-744-3370; www.chicagoblues festival.us

This three-day wail is the largest free blues fest on Earth, hosting icons of the genre from Chicago and beyond. Past performers include Ray Charles, BB King and Bonnie Raitt.

Fiestas Puertorriqueñas & Parade

☎ 773-292-1414

A huge parade, carnival rides and pork-filled eats bring millions to party with Chicago's Puerto Rican community in Humboldt Park.

Grant Park Music Festival

☎ 312-742-7638; www.grantpark musicfestival.com

The free, open-air orchestral programs at Millennium Park are an idyllic summer tradition, best accompanied by a bottle of wine.

Taste of Chicago

☎ 312-744-3370; www.tasteof chicago.us

The city's biggest festival draws hordes for a smorgasbord of excellent ethnic and local edibles.

Magical illuminated orbs signal Christmas mania during the Magnificent Mile Lights Festival (p26)

JULY

Chicago Outdoor Film Festival

☎ 312-774-3370; www.chicagoout
doorfilmfestival.us

From mid-July to the end of August, Grant Park screens classics under the stars.

Pitchfork Music Festival

☎ 312-744-3315; www.pitchfork
musicfestival.com

Bring a blanket and open ears for a weekend festival of taste-making underground rock.

Venetian Night

☎ 312-744-3370; www.venetiannight
chicago.us

This long-running annual floating parade lights up the lakeshore with twinkling boats and fireworks.

AUGUST

Bud Billiken Parade

☎ 877-244-2246; www.budbillikenpa
rade.com

On the second Saturday of August, the country's largest African American parade sends drill teams and brass bands stomping down Martin Luther King Jr Dr.

Lollapalooza

☎ 888-512-7469; www.lollapalooza.com

Though no longer a traveling show, this feisty hometown franchise is just as raucous as ever, bringing in heavy hitters such as Radiohead and Wilco.

SEPTEMBER

Chicago Jazz Fest

☎ 312-744-3370; www.chicagojazz
festival.us

The Labor Day weekend swings with jazz greats during Grant Park's free celebration.

Chicago World Music Festival

☎ 312-742-1938

A week of concerts, live radio broadcasts and in-store performances brings hundreds of contemporary and traditional jams from around the globe.

German-American Festival

☎ 630-653-3018; www.germanday.com

Don the lederhosen and raise a frothy stein at this annual Lincoln Plaza party.

CHICAGO SUMMER BLOCK PARTIES

> May: Chicago Mayfest, Lincoln Park
> June: Midsommarfest, Andersonville
> July: Fiesta Del Sol, Pilsen
> July: Old St Pat's World's Largest Block Party, West Loop
> July: Wicker Park Fest, Wicker Park
> August: Retro On Roscoe, Roscoe Village
> August: Northalsted Market Days, Lincoln Park

OCTOBER

Chicago Book Festival

☎ 312-747-4999; www.chicagopublic
libraryfoundation.org
The Chicago Public Library organizes readings, lectures and bookish citywide events
throughout the month.

Chicago Country Music Festival

☎ 312-744-3370; www.chicagocountry
musicfestival.us
From old-school icons, such as Loretta
and Waylon, to Nashville young 'uns, this
popular annual event (formerly held in
June) attracts country fans from miles and
miles around.

NOVEMBER

Chicago Humanities Festival

☎ 312-661-1028; www.chfestival.org
Chicago's 'festival of ideas' brings poets,
policy-makers and humanitarians for a
series of thought-provoking events.

Magnificent Mile Lights Festival

www.magnificentmilelightsfestival.com
A million lights accompany ringing cash
registers as music, Mickey Mouse and
fireworks bring Christmas mania.

Thanksgiving Parade

☎ 312-781-5681; www.chicago
festivals.org
Around 400,000 shivering souls watch local
celebrities and giant balloon animals float
down State St.

DECEMBER

Winter Wonderfest at Navy Pier

☎ 312-595-7437; www.navypier.com
With ice skating, rides and an eye-popping
indoor display, Chicago's most popular tourist
attraction goes all out for the holidays.

ZooLights

☎ 312-742-2000; www.lpzoo.org
As if the predatory cats weren't interesting
enough, Lincoln Zoo gets gussied up for the
holidays with sparkling trees, Santa spotting
and seasonal displays.

>ITINERARIES

A landmark in the Loop...and all that jazz, Chicago Theatre (p40)

ITINERARIES

Certain banner attractions in Chicago – such as the Art Institute, the Field Museum and the architectural splendors – could take days to explore in their fullest, but if time is limited, have no fear! Here are some options to follow in order to return home with a full-flavored taste of the Windy City.

DAY ONE

If you have only one day in Chicago, start by strolling through Chicago's showpiece, Millennium Park (p41). Sweep through the Art Institute of Chicago (p37) before hefting a slice of Giordano's (p55) deep-dish for lunch. Then, work it off on one of Chicago Architecture Foundation's walking tours (p42), pausing to snap a photo in front of Picasso's *Untitled* (Map pp38–9) and browsing aisles at the Jazz Record Mart (p53). Make time to catch the sunset from atop the Sears Tower (p41) and dine at Frontera Grill (p54), before downing a few pints at the Billy Goat Tavern (p53) and a late set at Buddy Guy's Legends (p138).

DAY TWO

Get thee to Wrigley Field (p79) to cheer on the Cubs (they'll need it). Wander past Wrigleyville's high-fiving sports bars and shops, then make a one-of-a-kind Chicago T-shirt at Strange Cargo (p83) before hitting 'the crotch' – the Wicker Park neighborhood at the intersection of North, Damen and Milwaukee Aves – where you can shop at boutiques, have highbrow libations at the Violet Hour (p109) and scarf down Chicago's signature take on tubular meat at Underdog (p107).

DAY THREE

On the third day, pay a call to Sue at the Field Museum (p131) and wander through Chinatown to grab some udon at Joy Yee's Noodle Shop (p135). Spend the afternoon walking the River North Gallery District (p166) or taking a ride on Navy Pier's breathtaking Ferris wheel (p49). For dinner, try a burly martini and slab of steak at Gibson's (p64) before catching the late show at Second City (p77).

Top left Hipster shopping heaven at Strange Cargo (p83), Wrigleyville **Top right** Friends enjoying a quiet beer at moody and intimate Danny's (p108), Bucktown **Bottom** A friendly welcome, aka Sue the *T rex*, at the Field Museum (p131)

WINTER DAY

When it's freezing – as in about half the year – meander the polished corridors of the Art Institute (p37) or Shedd Aquarium (p135). If you're willing to brave the cold, do some skating at the McCormick Tribune Ice Rink in Millennium Park (p47). After nightfall, do as the locals do, and make your way to the nearest tavern for a little liquid warm-up.

SUMMER DAY

Rent some wheels at Bike Chicago (p45) and see the city at a leisurely pace, picking up picnic supplies at one of the city's many farmers markets (www.chicagofarmersmarkets.us), such as the one on Thursday in Daley Plaza (Map pp38–9, D3), before catching a neighborhood festival (p21) or rolling up lakeshore to the 12th Street Beach. At sunset, bite into a heavy-metal-themed hamburger on the patio at Kuma's Corner (p117) or catch a classic flick under the stars at the Outdoor Film Festival (p25). Cap the night with cold Old Styles at one of the many neighborhood pubs with outdoor seating in Ukrainian Village (p108).

Keep snug on a winter's day at one of the many cozy neighborhood cafés

FORWARD PLANNING

Three weeks before you go Book a kitchen table at Charlie Trotter's (p73), and reserve tickets at Steppenwolf (p77), a Cub's game or Chicago Public Radio's fun quiz show *Wait, Wait Don't Tell Me* (below). Read the website of the Mayor's Office of Events (www .cityofchicago.org/specialevents) about big civic festivities that usually don't cost a thing. Pick up a copy of a Chicago tome, such as Erik Larson's *Devil in the White City* or Nelson Algren's *Chicago: City on the Make*.

One week before you go Dig through the online listings of the *Chicago Reader* (www .chicagoreader.com) to see who's going to take the stage at intimate venues such as the Hideout (p110), Schubas (p91) or the Green Mill (p99). Look over special exhibits and free lectures at the Art Institute (www.artic.edu) and the Field Museum (www.fieldmuseum.org). Download a do-it-yourself audio tour of Millennium Park for your iPod (www.antennaaudio .com/millenniumpark.shtml).

The day before you go Read some of the blogs at Chicagoist.com and the roster at www .chicagoblogmap.com to see what the city is talking about. Get hip to local news and the latest in Chicago politics by listening to WBEZ Chicago Public Radio at www.wbez.org. Check the weather for visibility from the Sears Tower Skydeck and adjust your packing; if Chicago's cutting wind doesn't get you, the wilting humidity just might.

FOR FREE

In addition to numerous free festivals (p21) throughout the warm months, growling back at the lions at the Lincoln Park Zoo (p69) is the best experience for spendthrift visitors. To dodge the price tag of the bird's-eye view from the Sears Tower, go to the Signature Room at the 95th in the Hancock Building (p65; the best view is from the ladies room), where the same view of the city doesn't cost a thing. With advance planning, you can catch a free taping of a quintessential Chicago broadcast: blockbusters such as Oprah or Springer, or hipper alternatives including public access indie rock kiddie dance party *Chic-a-Go-Go* or National Public Radio's *Wait, Wait Don't Tell Me* (www.npr.org/programs/waitwait/).

>NEIGHBORHOODS

The diamond lights of Chicago at twilight

NEIGHBORHOODS

Chicago's claim as a 'city of neighborhoods' is born out for all the senses – from the buttered smell of Swedish pastries that hangs over Andersonville to the scent of chocolate that wafts over the Clark St bridge.

Then there's the screeching calamity of the Loop and the leafy shush of Obama's old digs in Hyde Park, the smoky savor of ribs on the South Side or tangy flaming cheese in Greektown. The El clatters past roaring sports fans in Wrigleyville, pram-pushing yuppies in Lincoln Park and cinnamon-scented churro vendors in Pilsen. Blood sausage hangs in shop windows in the Ukrainian Village, Prada handbags in the boutiques of the Gold Coast. The unyielding tides of urban development, gentrification and immigration that are rapidly changing neighborhoods such as Pilsen have been at work elsewhere in town since the beginning, and this brilliant, messy, vibrant patchwork is the essence of Chicago.

Many banner attractions are clustered in the Loop, where the city's historic and business center is circled by train tracks (hence the name), or a few blocks away, in the Near North, where Magnificent Mile shops and eateries beg for travelers' attention (and dollars). But see only these neighborhoods and you'd be remiss: beyond the favorite sights is the real Chicago, with galleries, shops and architectural wonders, and an endless variety of dive bars and diners.

Getting around is easy if you understand the simple city plan. Chicago's streets are laid out in a numbered grid; Madison and State Sts in the Loop are at the grid's center. As you go north, south, east or west, each street number increases by 800 for every mile. Every increase of 400 is a major arterial street. For instance, Division St (1200 N) is followed by North Ave (1600 N) and Armitage Ave (2000 N), at which point you're 2.5 miles north of downtown.

Got it? Good. Now let's get moving.

LAKEWOOD-
BALMORAL

ANDERSONVILLE

ANDERSONVILLE,
LINCOLN SQUARE
& UPTOWN p93

Lake Michigan

WRIGLEYVILLE

LAKE VIEW &
WRIGLEYVILLE
pp80–1

LAKE VIEW

BUCKTOWN

LOGAN SQUARE &
HUMBOLDT PARK
p113

LINCOLN PARK &
OLD TOWN pp70–1

WICKER PARK   OLD TOWN

WICKER PARK, BUCKTOWN &
UKRAINIAN VILLAGE
pp102–3

GOLD COAST
pp60–1

STREETVILLE

UKRAINIAN
VILLAGE

NEAR NORTH

NEAR NORTH & NAVY
PIER pp50–1

ILLINOIS CENTER

GREEK TOWN

THE LOOP
pp38–9

PRINTER'S ROW

NEAR WEST SIDE &
PILSEN p121

LITTLE
ITALY

SOUTH LOOP & NEAR
SOUTH SIDE pp132–3

MUSEUM
CAMPUS

PILSEN

CHINATOWN

CERO

BRONZEVILLE

BRIDEPORT

KENWOOD

HYDE PARK &
SOUTH SIDE
p141

0   5 km
0   2 miles

>THE LOOP

You can't miss the Loop: this is the center of the action, where the pin-stripe mafia rushes the sidewalks and the machine-gun clatter of El trains echoes against the nation's first skyscrapers, where street traffic snarls and foot traffic hustles through a hectic grid of streets. But the Loop isn't all work and no play; this is the center of Chicago's humming tourism hub too. The city's regal old theaters light up with Broadway productions, the park-lined shores of Lake Michigan offer reprieve from the rush, and Millennium Park unfolds its whimsical offerings for everything from Schubert symphonies to splashing kiddies. There's plenty more peace and quiet to be had along the marble corridors of the Art Institute of Chicago, a city unto itself of fine art and artifacts, which demands a slice of any visitor's attention. Sights and accommodations are many, but restaurants in the Loop tend toward quick, cheap eats to satisfy the desk jockeys, or pricey expense account joints for their bosses.

THE LOOP

◉ SEE
Art Institute of Chicago	**1**	F4
Chicago	**2**	D3
Chicago Cultural Center	**3**	E2
Chicago Theatre	**4**	E2
Cloud Gate	**5**	F3
Crown Fountain	**6**	E3
Flamingo	**7**	D4
Four Seasons	**8**	D3
Harold Washington Library Center	**9**	D5
Lurie Garden	**10**	F3
Millennium Park	**11**	F3
Monument with Standing Beast	**12**	D2
Route 66 Sign	**13**	E4
Sears Tower	**14**	B4
Untitled	**15**	D3

🛍 SHOP
5 S Wabash Ave	**16**	E3
Chicago Architecture Foundation Shop	**17**	E4
Illinois Artisans Shop	**18**	C2
Iwan Ries & Company	**19**	E3
Prairie Avenue Bookshop	**20**	E5

🍴 EAT
Bombon	**21**	C3
Gage	**22**	E3
Gold Coast Dogs	**23**	E3
Italian Village	**24**	D4
Rhapsody	**25**	E4
Taza	**26**	B2

🍸 DRINK
17 West at the Berghoff	**27**	D4
Cal's Bar	**28**	C5

⭐ PLAY
Bike Chicago Millennium Park	**29**	F2
Chicago Symphony Orchestra	**30**	E4
Civic Opera House	**31**	B3
Daley Bicentennial Plaza	**32**	G2
Goodman Theatre	**33**	D2
Hubbard St Dance Chicago	**34**	F2
Joffrey Ballet of Chicago	**35**	E5
Lyric Opera of Chicago	(see 31)	
McCormick Tribune Ice Rink	**36**	E3

Please see over for map

◉ SEE

◉ ART INSTITUTE OF CHICAGO

☎ 312-443-3600; www.artic.edu/aic; 111 S Michigan Ave; adult/child $12/7, 5-8pm Thu & Fri admission free; ⏰ 10:30am-5pm Mon-Wed, 10:30am-9pm Thu & Fri, 10am-5pm Sat & Sun, shorter evening hours in winter; Ⓜ Brown, Green, Orange or Purple Line to Adams

Beyond the iconic bronze lions and up the grand staircase, the Art Institute of Chicago boasts one of the premiere fine-art collections of the world, with a particularly strong gathering of old masters, American painters and impressionists (the place is downright cluttered with Monet). The collection, which covers historic periods from ancient Egyptian, Greek, Roman and Asian art, has a cool collection of arms and armor and the breathtaking, newly opened Modern Wing. To help get your bearings, rent an audio tour ($6 – the Director's Tour will guide you to 40 popular masterpieces) or inquire about the frequent free lectures. To avoid the crowds, visit on Monday, or on a Thursday evening, when it's open late. See p14 for more on the institute.

◉ CHICAGO CULTURAL CENTER

☎ 312-744-6630; www.chicagoculturalcenter.org; 78 E Washington St; admission free; ⏰ 8am-7pm Mon-Thu,

Be impressed by the impressionists and so much more at the superb Art Institute of Chicago

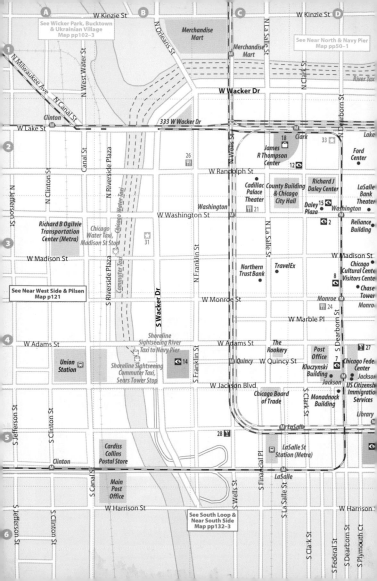

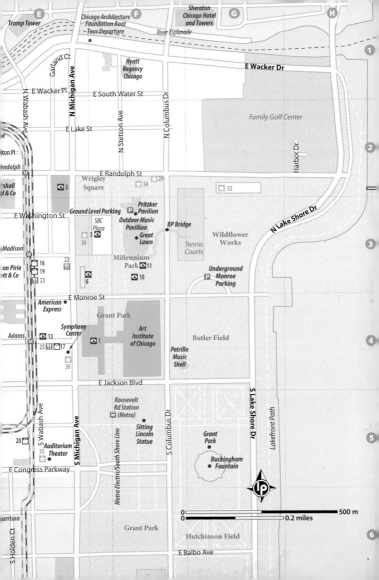

8am-6pm Fri, 9am-6pm Sat, 10am-6pm Sun; Ⓜ **Brown, Green, Orange or Purple Line to Randolph**
Originally built as the Chicago Public Library, this exquisite beaux arts building houses exhibitions, beautiful interior design and **lunchtime concerts** (admission free; ⏲ 12:15pm Mon-Fri). It contains two domes by Louis Comfort Tiffany, one of which is the world's largest (worth a cool $35 million), and the Chicago Office of Tourism. Excellent **tours** (☎ 312-742-1190; admission free; ⏲ 1:15pm Wed, Fri & Sat) leave from the Randolph St lobby.

Ⓒ CHICAGO THEATRE
☎ 312-462-6363; www.thechicagotheatre.com; 175 N State St; Ⓜ **Red Line to Lake**
Pose for a picture in front of this iconic theater, where everyone from Sinatra to Prince has performed (and left their signature

backstage). The opulent French baroque movie house, including a lobby modeled on the Palace of Versailles, originally opened in 1921. **Tours** ($5) are available Tuesdays year-round, Thursdays in summer and every third Saturday monthly. The marquee sign is an official landmark.

Ⓒ HAROLD WASHINGTON LIBRARY CENTER
☎ 312-747-4300; www.chicagopublic library.org; 400 S State St; admission free; ⏲ 9am-9pm Mon-Thu, 9am-5pm Fri & Sat, 1-5pm Sun; Ⓜ **Brown, Orange or Purple Line to Library**
This grand, art-filled building with free internet and wi-fi (get a temporary 'guest' card for access) is Chicago's fortresslike main library. Major authors give readings here, and exhibits constantly show in the galleries. The light-drenched, top-floor Winter Garden is a sweet

---

MASTERPIECES OF THE LOOP

> *Untitled,* Pablo Picasso (50 W Washington St) – the US Steel Works in Gary, Indiana, made this to Picasso's specifications and erected it in 1967.

> *Chicago,* Joan Miró (69 W Washington St) – this ceramic-covered 'great Earth mother' stands 39ft tall.

> *Monument with Standing Beast,* Jean Dubuffet (100 W Randolph St) – the white fiberglass work nicknamed 'Snoopy in a Blender' is constantly crawling with kids.

> *Four Seasons,* Marc Chagall (plaza at Dearborn and Monroe Sts) – in 1974 the Russian-born artist donated this mosaic – using thousands of bits of glass and stone – to the city.

> *Flamingo,* Alexander Calder (plaza at Dearborn and Adams Sts) – this soaring red structure provides much-needed relief from the stark facades of the federal building.

hideaway for reading, writing or just taking a load off, though it's a hike to get there.

◉ MILLENNIUM PARK
☎ 312-742-1168; www.millenn iumpark.org; Welcome Center, 201 E Randolph St; ⊙ 6am-11pm; Ⓜ Brown, Green, Orange or Purple Line to Randolph or Madison

Rising up boldly from Grant Park's northwest corner, Millennium Park is Chicago's civic showpiece, crowned by the Frank Gehry– designed Jay Pritzker Pavilion; Jaume Plensa's *Crown Fountain;* and Anish Kapoor's 110-ton, silver sculpture, *Cloud Gate,* known commonly as 'The Bean.' If the crowds at these attractions are too much, walk the peaceful Lurie Garden, where native plants pay homage to Illinois's tall-grass prairie. The Millennium Park Greeter Service offers free walking **tours** (⊙ 11:30am & 1pm) in summer. See p10 for more about the park.

◉ ROUTE 66 SIGN
Adams St btwn Michigan & Wabash Aves; Ⓜ Brown, Green, Orange or Purple Line to Adams

The so-called 'Main Street of America' starts right here, ending some 2500 miles later in LA. Look for the sign that marks the spot on Adams St's north side as you head west toward Wabash Ave.

The soaring Sears, still the tallest in the States

◉ SEARS TOWER
☎ 312-875-9696; www.the-sky deck.com; 233 S Wacker Dr; Skydeck admission adult/3-11yr $12.95/9.50; ⊙ 10am-10pm Apr-Sep, to 8pm Oct-Mar, last ticket sold 30min before closing; Ⓜ Brown, Orange or Purple Line to Quincy

Sure, the Sears Tower lost its claim as the world's tallest building some time ago, but the 110-story building remains the tallest in the US (at least until the Spire is completed). For those who prefer a cocktail with their vertigo – er, view – the John Hancock Center (p59) is a better choice and a free way to drink in the skyline.

🛍 SHOP

🏠 5 S WABASH AVE *Jewelry*

5 S Wabash Ave; 🕒 closed Sun; Ⓜ Brown, Green, Orange or Purple Line to Madison
In the heart of 'Jewelers Row,' this old building is the center of Chicago's family gem trade. Scores of shops and brokers sell every kind of watch, ring and gemstone imaginable and many are quick to promise wholesale.

🏠 CHICAGO ARCHITECTURE FOUNDATION SHOP
Souvenirs

☎ 312-922-3432; 224 S Michigan Ave; Ⓜ Brown, Green, Orange or Purple Line to Adams

Chicago Architecture Foundation Shop

This excellent shop for only-in-Chicago type souvenirs is appropriately housed in a building by one of the city's architectural fathers, Daniel Burnham. You can pick up Frank Lloyd Wright paraphernalia and heaps of books to study the buildings around you. This is also the place to join one of the many architectural walking tours, or book a river tour, one of the city's best tourist experiences.

🏠 ILLINOIS ARTISANS SHOP
Arts & Crafts

☎ 312-814-5321; James R Thompson Center, 100 W Randolph St, 2nd fl; 🕒 closed Sat & Sun; Ⓜ Brown, Green, Orange, Purple or Blue Line to Clark
Excellent work by artisans from around the state is sold here, including ceramics, glass and wood coaxed into everything from fine jewelry to colorful toys. Best of all, the prices verge on cheap. The Illinois Art Gallery next door sells paintings and sculptures under the same arrangement.

🏠 IWAN RIES & COMPANY
Smoke Shop

☎ 800-621-1457; www.iwanries.com; 19 S Wabash Ave, 2nd fl; 🕒 9am-5:30pm Mon-Fri, to 5pm Sat; Ⓜ Brown, Green, Orange or Purple Line to Madison
Follow the sweet aroma up the stairs to this classic tobacconist,

on the 2nd floor of a downtown office building. It has over 12,000 pipes lining the walls, imported cigars and fine cigarettes, and sweet pouches of exotic tobacco.

🏛 PRAIRIE AVENUE BOOKSHOP *Bookstore*
☎ 312-922-8311; 418 S Wabash Ave; 🕑 closed Sun; Ⓜ Brown, Orange or Purple Line to Library

In the most lavishly decorated bookstore in the city, you'll find piles of beautiful architectural and historical tomes, including many hard-to-find titles.

🍴 EAT
🍴 BOMBON *Mexican* $
☎ 312-781-2788; www.bomboncafe.com; 170 W Washington St; mains $6-9; Ⓜ Brown, Orange or Purple Line to Washington

An offshoot of its revered Pilsen flagship, this bright café and bakery draws mobs of lunching workers for the array of *tortas* (Mexican sandwiches on thick, crusty bread). Die-hard sweet tooths should head straight for the bakery case, as the pastries are also renowned.

🍴 GAGE *American* $$
☎ 312-372-4243; www.thegagechicago.com; 24 S Michigan Ave; mains $10-38; Ⓜ Brown, Orange, Purple or Green Line to Adams

Just check out the formidable Scotch egg – a sausage-meat-encased, deep-fried, hard-boiled egg the girth of a softball – and you'll know that this elegant Loop gastro-pub menu is *serious*. The $16 (but worth it) 'Gage burger' and fish-and-chips plate beg to be washed down with one of the wide selection of pints. Or, for an earthy upscale option, go with the saddle of elk.

🍴 GOLD COAST DOGS *American* $
☎ 312-578-1133; 17 S Wabash Ave; mains $3-6; 🕑 to 6pm; Ⓜ Brown, Green, Orange or Purple Line to Madison

A good place in the Loop to sample the classic 'Chicago dog,' this humble café serves tubed pork with the city's elaborate dressing: onions, relish, mustard, hot peppers, celery salt and a pickle spear. (Do it like a local: no ketchup!) The surrounds are unsightly – it shares a space with a fast-food chain – but when the weather permits, take the dogs for a short walk to Millennium Park.

🍴 ITALIAN VILLAGE *Italian* $$$
☎ 312-332-7005; www.italianvillage-chicago.com; 71 W Monroe St; mains $15-35; 🕑 closed Sun; Ⓜ Blue Line to Monroe

Of the three restaurants under one roof, two are worth your while: the namesake Village, and Vivere. The former is decorated with the facades and twinkling lights of an Italian hill town – it's campy but cute – and has a menu of pasta and meat dishes served with traditional sauces. Vivere is the more creative cousin downstairs, offering a wide-ranging wine list that's some 1500 bottles strong. It was also a preferred site for Barack and Michelle Obama's 'date nights.'

¶¶ RHAPSODY American $$
☎ 312-786-9911; 65 E Adams St; mains $11-28; Ⓜ Brown, Green, Orange or Purple Line to Adams

Tucked inside Symphony Center, Rhapsody's dining room opens to a lovely garden – perfect for regaining your strength after a visit to the Art Institute, or filling up before Mahler. Menu highlights include the halibut with roasted artichokes and little neck clams, and succulent beef tenderloin. Some of the top-notch desserts even feature chocolate bits cleverly etched with gilded musical notes.

¶¶ TAZA Mediterranean $
☎ 312-201-9885; 176 N Franklin St; mains $4-7; Ⓨ lunch; Ⓜ Brown or Orange Line to Washington

The tiled floor and undressed tables don't overwhelm with ambi-

ence, but when it comes to the holy trinity of cheapie Mediterranean pita-wrapped staples – falafel, shawarma and gyro – this humble lunch joint is awe inspiring.

Ⓨ DRINK

Ⓨ 17 WEST AT THE BERGHOFF
Bar
☎ 312-427-3170; 17 W Adams St; Ⓨ 11am-9pm Mon-Thu, to 9:30pm Fri, 11:30am-10pm Sat; Ⓜ Blue Line to Jackson

This sleek replacement of the historic Berghoff Standup Bar is generally met with a grumble from locals set in their ways, but the food is reliable and the atmosphere retains much of the old charm. At lunch you'll probably have to fight your way through billing clerks with a hankering for roast beef.

Ⓨ CAL'S BAR Bar
☎ 312-922-6392; s400 S Wells St; Ⓨ 7am-8pm Sun-Wed, to 2am Thu-Sat; Ⓜ Blue Line to La Salle

The bartenders serve plenty of 'tude with the drinks at this family-owned dive and liquor store, which serves as a lone oasis for scruffy hipsters who find themselves misplaced among the pinstripes in the Loop. On weekends, punk-rock bands with names such as Broadzilla and Johnny Vomit take the stage.

⭐ PLAY
⭐ BIKE CHICAGO MILLENNIUM PARK
Bike Rental

☎ 888-245-3929; www.bikechicago
.com; 239 E Randolph St; per hr $8,
per day $30-35; ⏰ 6:30am-8pm Mon-
Fri, 8am-8pm Sat & Sun Jun-Aug, 6:30am-
7pm Mon-Fri, 9am-7pm Sat & Sun Apr-
May & Sep-Oct, 6:30am-6:30pm
Mon-Fri Nov-Mar; Ⓜ Brown, Green,
Orange or Purple Line to Randolph

Riding along the 18.5-mile long
Lakefront Bike Path is a great way
to see the city. Though there are
120 miles of bike lanes around
town, traffic can be less than re-
spectful, making street peddling a
bit more of a challenge. Request a
free bike map from the **City Department of Transportation** (www.chicago
bikes.org). You can arrange to pick a
bike up at one Bike Chicago location and drop off at another; reserve online and you save money.
Child seats and tandem bikes are
available, as are guided tours.

⭐ CHICAGO SYMPHONY ORCHESTRA *Orchestra*

☎ 312-294-3000; www.cso.org;
Symphony Center, 220 S Michigan Ave;
Ⓜ Brown, Green or Orange Line to
Adams

The city's fine orchestra is await-
ing its newest incarnation after
quickly losing promising young
director Daniel Barenboim. His
replacement, Italian conductor
Riccardo Muti, begins his contract
in 2010. The Chicago Symphony
Orchestra is among America's
best symphonies, and is known
for its fervent subscribers and an
untouchable brass section. The
season runs from September to
May, though the orchestra also
performs summer engagements
at **Ravinia** (www.ravinia.org).

⭐ GOODMAN THEATRE
Theater

☎ 312-443-3800; www.goodman
theatre.org; 170 N Dearborn St; Ⓜ Blue,
Brown, Green or Orange Line to Clark/Lake

Recognized among the best
regional theaters in the US, the
Goodman specializes in new and
classic American theater and has a
2008 Tony award for excellence in
regional theater among its many
accolades.

⭐ HUBBARD STREET DANCE CHICAGO *Modern Dance*

☎ 312-850-9744; www.hubbardstreet
dance.com; Harris Theater for Music &
Dance, 205 E Randolph Dr; Ⓜ Brown,
Green or Orange Line to Randolph

Hubbard Street is the preeminent
dance group in the city, with a
well-deserved international reputation. The group delivers

Christina Anthony

Second City Etc cast member, vet of venerated Chicago stages at the Goodman Theatre and Chicago Shakespeare Theater, and performer at Chicago Improv Festival and Chicago Sketchfest

Perfect day taking visiting friends to Chicago Hanging out in Wicker Park (p100), where I live, kind of a hipster 'hood, where you can visit the hot-dog stands and all the people look like they just stepped out of a rock video.
Quintessential Chicago theater experiences Second City (p77), of course! If you're into drama, an evening at Steppenwolf (p77) can be pretty amazing. The Neo-Futurists (p99), another company I perform with, is a really cool show, with a young crowd. **How to cope with Chicago in winter** Cry? Or maybe check out some great black box theater (see Lookingglass, p67), or go ice skating (opposite) in Millennium Park.

explosive and technical performances from the best choreographers in the world.

⭐ JOFFREY BALLET OF CHICAGO *Ballet*
☎ 312-739-0120; www.joffreyballet.org; Auditorium Theatre, 50 E Congress Pkwy; Ⓜ Brown or Orange Line to Library

Since relocating from New York in 1995, this group has overshadowed the city's civic ballet, with energetic work and an impressive storehouse of regular repertoire.

⭐ LYRIC OPERA OF CHICAGO *Opera*
☎ 312-332-2244; www.lyricopera .org; Civic Opera House, 20 N Wacker Dr; Ⓜ Brown or Orange Line to Washington

A premiere of William Bolcom's *A Wedding* (an adaptation of a Robert Altman movie) was an aptly bold celebration of the Lyric Opera's 50th anniversary. A truly great modern opera company, the seasons are popular with subscribers, who fill the ornate **Civic Opera House** (☎ 312-419-0033; www.civic operahouse.com; 20 N Wacker Dr).

⭐ MCCORMICK TRIBUNE ICE RINK *Ice Skating*
☎ 312-742-5222; 55 N Michigan Ave; skating free, skate rentals $5-7; ⏱ noon-9pm Mon-Thu, noon-10pm Fri, 10am-10pm Sat & Sun; Ⓜ Brown, Green, Orange or Purple Line to Randolph or Madison

In addition to this rink within Millennium Park, the Chicago Park District operates a first-class winter rink at **Daley Bicentennial Plaza** (☎ 312-742-7650; 337 E Randolph St). Admission is free to both; skate rental costs $5 to $7. They're open from late November to late February.

>NEAR NORTH & NAVY PIER

If the Loop is where Chicago fortunes are made, the Near North is where they're spent. People come here to swing their bags along the energetic sidewalks of the neighborhood's main drag, N Michigan Ave, known as the Magnificent Mile. Stretching from the Tribune Tower to the historic Water Tower, the route is silly with multistory malls and high-end department stores. It glows with majestic, fairy-tale warmth from mid-November through January, when the stores string up their twinkly holiday lights. Jutting off Near North's east end is Navy Pier, Chicago's biggest tourist attraction for families. It's a cavalcade of kid- and teen-oriented shops, rides and attractions, with a colossal Ferris wheel, though adults have opportunities for romantic, windswept strolling. It's about a 15-minute march from Michigan Ave. Just east of the Mile is the River North Gallery district, which claims the most concentrated cluster of galleries anywhere outside Manhattan.

NEAR NORTH & NAVY PIER

👁 SEE
Chicago Spire 1 F4
Chicago Water Taxi,
   Michigan Ave Stop 2 D4
Ferris Wheel 3 G4
Navy Pier 4 G4
Smith Museum of Stained
   Glass Windows 5 H4
Tribune Tower 6 D4

🏠 SHOP
Abraham Lincoln
   Book Shop 7 B3

Chicago Tribune
   Store ....(see 6)
Jazz Record Mart 8 D4

🍽 EAT
Billy Goat Tavern 9 D4
Frontera Grill 10 C4
Gene & Georgetti 11 B4
Gino's East 12 B3
Giordano's 13 D3
Mr Beef 14 B3
Pizzeria Uno 15 D4
Topolobampo ....(see 10)

🍸 DRINK
Brehon Pub 16 B3
Clark St Ale House 17 C3

⭐ PLAY
Blue Chicago 18 C4
Chicago Children's
   Museum 19 G4
River Esplanade 20 E4
Weird Chicago Tours ...21 C3

Please see over for map

◉ SEE

◉ MAGNIFICENT MILE

www.themagnificentmile.com; Michigan
Ave from the Chicago River north to Oak
St; Ⓜ Red Line to Grand

The mall-packed Magnificent
Mile is among the most illustrious shopping streets in the
world and its stats impress: the
district brings in over a billion
dollars every year, even if the
retailers are mostly high-end
department stores and chains
available elsewhere throughout
the country. The strip goes all
out in December, when treasure-
laden shoppers rush home under
holiday lights and adornments.

◉ NAVY PIER

☎ 312-595-7437; www.navypier
.com; 600 E Grand Ave; admission
free; ☼ 10am-10pm Sun-Thu, to
midnight Fri & Sat, earlier closing times
Sep-May; 🚌 124

Stretching away from the
skyline and into the blue of Lake
Michigan, the half-mile-long Navy
Pier may induce groans from
locals, but its brilliant views, fresh
breezes and family appeal make it
Chicago's most-visited attraction.
High-tech rides, splash fountains,
big boats and greasy snacks will
blow the minds of young ones. For
the childless, the charms revolve
around the views, especially from
the stomach-turning, 150ft Ferris

A sign of fun times ahead at Navy Pier

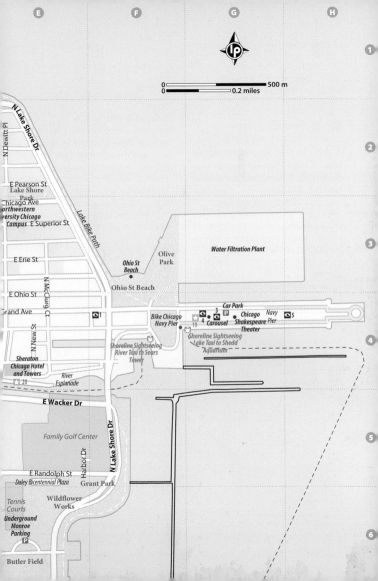

wheel (per ride $6). In summer, enjoy live music and fireworks weekly.

🔎 SMITH MUSEUM OF STAINED GLASS WINDOWS

☎ 312-595-5024; Navy Pier; admission free; 🕙 10am-10pm Sun-Thu, to midnight Fri & Sat, earlier closing times Sep-May; 🚌 124

This free, quietly impressive attraction on the lower-level terraces of Navy Pier's Festival Hall is the country's first museum dedicated entirely to stained glass. Many of the 150 pieces on display were made in Chicago and hung in area churches, homes and office buildings. Fans of Louis Comfort Tiffany will marvel at his 13 works.

🔎 TRIBUNE TOWER

435 N Michigan Ave; Ⓜ Red Line to Grand

Colonel Robert McCormick, eccentric owner of the *Tribune,* collected pieces of famous buildings and monuments from around the world. Embedded around the Tower's base are chunks of the Taj Mahal, the Great Pyramid and hundreds of other momentous buildings, including wreckage from the World Trade Center.

🛍 SHOP

📖 ABRAHAM LINCOLN BOOK SHOP *Bookstore*

☎ 312-944-3085; 357 W Chicago Ave; 🕙 closed Sun; Ⓜ Brown or Purple Line to Chicago

THE DOWNWARD SPIRE

It seems that the grand schemes of Chicago's architectural founding father Daniel Burnham were still ringing in Santiago Calatrava's ears when he drew up plans for the Chicago Spire, a building that captivated Chicagoans when it was unveiled in 2005. It wasn't just the audacious design (its twisting shape resembling a giant unicorn's horn) or the gargantuan size (its estimated 2000ft would dwarf the Sears Tower), Calatrava's design was ambitious in the details, employing Frank Lloyd Wright's concept of 'total design' right down to the doorknobs. Though derogatory nicknames for the building immediately buzzed around town ('The Twizzler', 'The Drill Bit' among them), the building enjoyed wide public support when ground was broken in 2007. It hardly went racing toward the heavens though: construction came screeching to a halt in the fall of 2008 due to lack of funds, leaving a dormant 76ft-deep, 110ft-wide hole in the middle of some of the city's most valuable real estate. Though the developers blame the lack of cash on the wider financial crisis in the US, they vow to finish the project. If the Spire is completed, it will become the tallest building in America and another jewel in Chicago's encrusted skyline. If it doesn't, it might live up to one of its less savory nicknames: 'The Big Screw.'

This hushed, museumlike shop carries new, used and antiquarian books about Illinois' *other* historic president, Honest Abe. If you want a real, Lincoln-signed White House memo, and have a cool $30,000 burning a hole in your pocket, you've come to the right place.

 CHICAGO TRIBUNE STORE
Souvenirs

☎ 312-222-3080; Tribune Tower, 435 N Michigan Ave; ☒ closed Sun; Ⓜ Red Line to Grand

While this small store doesn't have the selection of other souvenir places in Chicago, its collection of Tribune-related merchandise is desirable. Cubs hats and jerseys, and books by noted Chicago authors are also available.

☐ JAZZ RECORD MART
Record Shop

☎ 312-222-1467; 27 E Illinois St; Ⓜ Red Line to Grand

You have to hunt for this revered place – it's below street level, right on the river – but jazzheads, blues aficionados and vintage vinyl collectors seek it out, as it makes the short list of best record stores in the nation. You can spend hours fingering through the rows of dusty LPs or chatting up owner Bob Koester and his dedicated staff about local blues and jazz. Fans of Chicago blues should stop

For serious music heads only: Jazz Record Mart

for a meaningful aural souvenir, especially from the shop's boutique label, Delmark.

🍴 EAT

🍴 BILLY GOAT TAVERN
American $

☎ 312-222-1525; www.billygoattavern .com; lower level, 430 N Michigan Ave; mains $3-6; Ⓜ Red Line to Grand

Literally beneath the pie-eyed mobs on the Magnificent Mile, the Billy Goat, which enjoyed the fame of John Belushi's *Saturday Night Live* skit ('Cheezborger! Cheezborger!'), remains a deserving tourist magnate. Skip the franchise locations for the original – a

'No fries, cheeps! No Pepsi, Coke!' John Belushi's beloved Billy Goat Tavern (p53)

windowless subterranean haunt with famously cantankerous Greeks and scads of old-Chicago charm. Most importantly, remember – 'No fries, cheeps! No Pepsi, Coke!'

🍴 FRONTERA GRILL
Mexican $$
☎ 312-661-1434; 445 N Clark St; mains $14-25; ⏱ closed Sun; Ⓜ Red Line to Grand

Cluttered with folk art, this is the best source for celebrity Rick Bayless' fresh south-of-the-border inspirations. Warm tortillas are made on site for tacos al carbón, filled with charred beef and grilled green onions. The place attracts a

colorful crowd, so expect a wait; reservations are only taken for five or more. For Bayless' creativity unleashed (and a higher price), go next door to **Topolobampo** (☎ 312-661-1434; 445 North Clark St; ⏱ 11:45am-2pm Tue, 11:30am-2pm Wed-Fri, 5:30-9:30pm Tue-Thu, 5:30-10:30pm Fri & Sat); see p144 for a description of what the Obamas ate when they dined here.

🍴 GENE & GEORGETTI
American $$$
☎ 312-527-3718; 500 N Franklin St; mains $15-35; ⏱ closed Sun; Ⓜ Brown Line to Merchandise Mart

Chicago's oldest steak house boasts signed photos by Sinatra and Lucille Ball and solid Italian fare. Old-timers, politicos and regulars are seated downstairs. New-timers, conventioneers and tourists are seated upstairs. The steaks are the same on either level: thick, well aged and well priced.

GINO'S EAST *Pizza* $$

☎ 312-943-1124; 633 N Wells St; mains $7-25; Ⓜ Brown Line to Chicago

Leave your name on the graffiti-covered walls of this deep-dish superpower while shoveling down classic slices of cheese-and-sausage pie in a crispy cornmeal crust.

GIORDANO'S *Pizza* $$

☎ 312-951-0747; 730 N Rush St; mains $8-26; Ⓜ Red Line to Chicago

The founders of this local chain got their winning recipe for stuffed pizza from – aww – their momma back in Italy. If you want a slice of heaven, order the 'special,' a pizza stuffed with sausage, mushroom, green pepper and onions.

PIZZA TO GO...FAR

To return home with the ultimate edible Chicago souvenir, try shipping home a deep-dish pizza. A couple of the best pizzerias in town pack their famous pies on dry ice and ship them anywhere in the USA. Look to **Giordano's** (☎ 800-982-1756; www.giordanos.com) or **Gino's East** (☎ 800-344-5455; www.ginoseast.com), where you can get some serious pizza way back home for roughly $25, plus about $25 more for shipping.

MR BEEF *American* $

☎ 312-337-8500; 660 N Orleans St; mains $4-7; lunch, closed Sun; Ⓜ Brown Line to Chicago

At this local classic, the $5 Italian beef sandwiches come with long, spongy white buns that rapidly go soggy after a load of the spicy beef and cooking juices has been ladled on.

PIZZERIA UNO *Pizza* $$

☎ 312-321-1000; 29 E Ohio St; mains $8-26; Ⓜ Red Line to Grand

Ike Sewell supposedly invented Chicago-style pizza at this cozy tourist juggernaut in 1943, although his claim inspires debate among locals. A light, flaky crust holds piles of cheese and a herbed tomato sauce. The $18 classic lands on the table with a resounding thud and can feed a family of four.

DRINK

BREHON PUB *Pub*

☎ 312-642-1071; 731 N Wells St; 11am-2am Mon-Fri, noon-3am Sat, noon-2am Sun; Ⓜ Brown Line to Chicago

This Irish stalwart is a fine example of the corner saloons that once dotted the city. The ample selection of draft beer in frosted

Let your littlun's imagination run wild at the Chicago Children's Museum

glasses is served to neighborhood crowds perched on the high stools.

CLARK ST ALE HOUSE Pub
☎ 312-642-9253; 742 N Clark St;
🕐 4pm-4am Mon-Thu, to 5am Fri & Sat, to 2am Sun; Ⓜ Red Line to Chicago
With the Near North's best beer selection, you can sample the Midwest's finest microbrews out back in the courtyard. An excellent place to spend an afternoon.

★ PLAY

★ BLUE CHICAGO Blues Club
☎ 312-642-6261; www.bluechicago .com; 736 N Clark St; Ⓜ Red Line to Chicago

If you're staying in the neighborhood and don't feel like hitting the road, you won't go wrong at this mainstream blues club. Admission also gets you into two nearby branches.

★ CHICAGO CHILDREN'S MUSEUM Museum
☎ 312-527-1000; www.chichildrensm useum.org; Navy Pier; admission $8, Thu after 5pm free; 🕐 10am-5pm Sun-Wed & Fri, to 8pm Thu & Sat; 🚌 124
Designed as an imagination workout for the 10-and-under set, the chipper museum near the main entrance to Navy Pier gives its wee visitors enough hands-on exhibits to keep them climbing

and creating for hours. There's a highly contentious proposal to move the museum to Grant Park, though at press time they hadn't broken ground.

⭐ RIVER ESPLANADE *Walk*
Chicago River waterfront, btwn N Michigan Ave & N McClurg Ct
An excellent place to escape the manic bustle of the 'Mag Mile,' the River Esplanade sweeps along the river bank in the shadows of downtown steel giants. The huge arc of water erupting from the Central Fountain commemorates the labor-intensive reversal of the Chicago River in 1900.

⭐ WEIRD CHICAGO TOURS *Tour*
☎ 888-446-7859; www.weirdchicago .com; most tours depart cnr N Clark & W Ontario Sts; adult/child $30/20; ⏱ call for schedule
These three-hour bus tours, presented by a droll staff of former class clowns, offer the perfect trifecta of spirited history lessons, corny jokes and paranormal gabble. The adults-only 'Red Light District Sex Tour' is a blast.

>GOLD COAST

The retail-driven madness of the Near North starts to change as you enter an anomaly in America's proudest blue-collar city: the moneyed enclave of the Gold Coast. This, Chicago's richest neighborhood, outshines even its gilded name. A stroll past the hushed, tree-lined streets and historic mansions in the Astor St area provides a glimpse into Chicago's wealthy past. An afternoon in the quaint shops of luxuriant designer wares or an evening among the glittering high heels and good cheekbones of the neighborhood's nightlife is an ample introduction to its moneyed present. On Friday night, see-and-be-seen crowds glide through bars and restaurants at Rush and State Sts, where businessmen carve porterhouses while downing martinis and ogling the action – no wonder locals call the area the 'Viagra Triangle.' For window-shopping and people-watching, Chicago offers no finer spectacle. Further away from the lake to the west, grit overtakes glitz, especially around the former site of the Cabrini-Green housing project, once the city's most bleak. Today it's being demolished, and its residents relocated to the Chicago suburbs, far from tourists' eyes.

GOLD COAST

◉ SEE

⬒ SHOP

🍴 EAT

🍷 DRINK

★ PLAY

Please see over for map

👁 SEE

🔵 INTERNATIONAL MUSEUM OF SURGICAL SCIENCE

☎ 312-642-6502; www.imss.org; 1524 N Lake Shore Dr; adult/student $8/4, Tue admission free; 🕐 10am-4pm Tue-Sun May-Sep, closed Sun Oct-Apr; 🚌 151, Ⓜ Red Line to Clark/Division

Home to an eclectic (and sometimes chilling) collection of surgical gear, the Museum of Surgical Science has fascinating thematic displays, such as the one on bloodletting. An amazing collection of 'stones' (as in 'kidney' and 'gall-') and the somewhat alarming ancient Roman vaginal speculum leave lasting impressions.

🔵 JOHN HANCOCK CENTER

☎ 312-751-3681; www.hancock -observatory.com; 875 N Michigan Ave; adult/5-12yr $15/9; 🕐 9am-11pm; Ⓜ Red Line to Chicago

Though less popular than the Sears Tower's Skydeck, the Hancock's viewing platform includes benefits such as shorter lines, fresh air and an arguably superior view, some 94 floors above Lake Michigan. But only a sucker would pay for the windy observation area when you can take a free ride to the Hancock's 96th-floor Signature Lounge where you can spend the same amount on an overpriced cocktail to accompany the view.

🔵 MUSEUM OF CONTEMPORARY ART

☎ 312-280-2660; www.mcachicago.org; 220 E Chicago Ave; adult/student $12/7, Tue admission free; 🕐 10am-8pm Tue, to 5pm Wed-Sun; Ⓜ Red Line to Chicago

Within the somewhat imposing, mesh-encased MCA building you'll find surprisingly bright hallways and an especially strong minimalist, surrealist and book arts collection. The permanent collection includes works by Franz Kline, René Magritte, Cindy Sherman and Andy Warhol. It also regularly hosts dance, film and speaking events from an international array of contemporary artists. There are free daily tours and A-list traveling exhibits.

🔵 WATER TOWER

806 N Michigan Ave; Ⓜ Red Line to Chicago

Sure, Oscar Wilde famously called it a 'castellated monstrosity,' but the 1869 limestone Water Tower and its associated building, the Pumping Station, were the only monsters left after the 1871 fire. The structure never worked too well – the water intake cribs in Lake Michigan brought both fish and sewage to people's taps – but public outcry has prevented its demolition. Today it's home to an excellent **City Gallery** (☎ 312-742-0808; admission free; 🕐 10am-6:30pm Mon-Sat, to 5pm Sun),

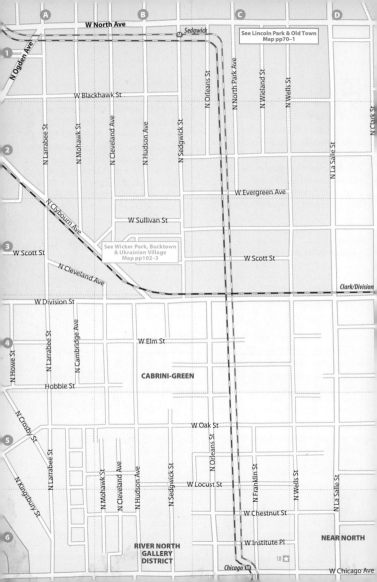

E

W North Ave

F

Lake Shore Dr

G

H

⊙ 1

0 _____ 400 m
0 _____ 0.2 miles

N Dearborn St

N State St

N Astor St

W Schiller St

E Banks St

OLD COAST

14 ⑭

W Goethe St

Lake Bike Path

Lake Michigan

22 ⑮

E Scott St

13 ⑯

E Division St

15 ⑰ 20 ⑱

9 ⑲

E Elm St

21 ⑳ Oak St
Beach

10 ⑩

E Cedar St

W Maple St

12 ⑫

E Bellevue Pl

N Lake Shore Dr

11 ⑪

16 ⑯

E Oak St

8 ⑧

E Lake Shore Dr

19 ⑲

N Rush St

E Walton St

17 ⑰

5 ⑤

N Dewitt Pl

shington
quare St

E Delaware Pl

N Michigan Ave

*The
Viagra
Triangle*

N State St

2 ⑫

N Wabash St

E Chestnut St

N Dearborn St

*Water Works
Pumping Station;
Water Works
Visitor Center*

6 ⑥ *Water Town
Place*

W Chestnut St

E Pearson St

E Pearson St

4 ⑭ 7 ⑦

Seneca
Park

3 ⑬

Lake Shore Park

Ⓜ Chicago

E Chicago Ave

with Chicago-themed works and blessed sanctuary from the surrounding Mag Mile madness.

SHOP

900 N MICHIGAN
Shopping Mall

☎ 312-915-3916; www.shop900.com; 900 N Michigan Ave; Ⓜ Red Line to Chicago

Like many of the other malls on this stretch, this elegant six-story commercial emporium has a fair share of common retailers, but this address brings together the most luxurious names – Bloomingdale's, Gucci etc – under one roof. In short, it's why plastic was invented.

AMERICAN GIRL PLACE
Toyshop

☎ 877-247-5223; www.americangirl .com; 835 N Michigan Ave; Ⓜ Red Line to Chicago

Settling into larger digs at the Water Tower Place (yet another mall on the Magnificent Mile), this is not your mother's doll shop; it's an *experience*. Here, dolls are treated as real people: the 'hospital' carts them away in wheelchairs for repairs; the café seats the dolls as part of the family during tea service; and the dolls' owners – usually outfitted in matching threads, naturally – take classes with their little pals. Creepy? Maybe a little, but the fact that the average shopper's visit lasts three hours is a testament to the immersive environment.

CITY OF CHICAGO STORE
Souvenirs

☎ 312-742-8811; www.chicagostore .com; Water Works Visitor Center, 163 E Pearson St; Ⓜ Red Line to Chicago

Purchase authentic pieces of the city, from decommissioned city parking meters ($175) to street signs for famous local streets

WHAT'S IN A NAME? OR WHERE?

Chicago loves to give colorful nicknames to its people, places and things. Here's a handy translation of the colorful Chicagoese.

> Cheesehead – Chicago's nickname for its Wisconsin neighbors to the north.
> The Crotch – the intersection of North, Damen and Milwaukee Aves in Wicker Park.
> Pop – in Chicago, soda is called by no other name.
> Trixies and Chads – derogatory hipster shorthand for well-groomed, well-heeled scene makers.
> The Viagra Triangle – the triangle of streets made up by Chicago Ave and State and Rush Sts, where mature gentlemen seek youthful companionship.

A glimpse into Chicago's moneyed past, Astor St

($50). There's a lot of the typical miscellany too, such as pint-sized replicas of the city's big buildings.

🄲 DENIM LOUNGE
Clothing & Accessories
☎ 312-642-6403; 43 E Oak St; Ⓜ Red Line to Clark/Division
There are miles of the namesake material in this friendly basement-level store, where men and women can find the holy grail of perfect fitting jeans with the aid of a four-dimensional fitting station.

🄲 FLIGHT 001 *Travel*
☎ 312-944-1001; www.flight001 .com; 1133 N State St; Ⓜ Red Line to Clark/Division

The brightly colored hard-shelled luggage and stock of travel gadgets will get a rise out of any would-be jetsetter. The store is sleek as can be; you even get cashed out at a retro airline ticket counter.

🍴 EAT
🍴 ASHKENAZ *Kosher Deli* $$
☎ 312-944-5006; 12 E Cedar St; mains $8-15; Ⓜ Red Line to Chicago
There aren't too many kosher delis in Chicago, but the thick stacks of corned beef and pastrami and briny pickles that come from Ashkenaz can hold their own west of New York. Also, among the pricey options and chains of the

Gold Coast, it has the best quick, cheapie lunch.

🍴 FOODLIFE *Eclectic* $
☎ 312-787-7100; www.foodlifechicago .com; 835 N Michigan Ave; mains $5-10; 🕐 7:30am-8pm Mon-Fri, 11am-9pm Sat & Sun; Ⓜ Red Line to Chicago; Ⓥ

'Call it a restaurant. Call it an eatery. Just don't call it a food court!' demands the mantra of Foodlife – a place with over a dozen different globally themed kitchens featuring fresh, gourmet, à la carte options in a sleek atmosphere. Even if you call it a you-know-what, it might be the most wondrous one you've ever visited, with a bazaar of ethnic-fusion cuisine and plenty of good options for vegetarians. Situated inside the Water Tower Place shopping center, it's ideal for gangs of indecisive shoppers.

🍴 GIBSON'S
Steak House $$$
☎ 312-266-8999; 1028 N Rush St; mains $20-80; 🕐 closed lunch Mon-Thu; Ⓜ Red Line to Clark/Division

With its perch at the heart of the Rush St action, politicos, scene makers and after-work prowlers compete for prime table space in the buzzing dining area. The bar is a prime stalking place for available millionaires. As for the meat on the plates, the steaks are as good as

they come, sold to you by a surly staff of waiters.

🍴 ORIGINAL PANCAKE HOUSE
Breakfast $
☎ 312-642-7917; 22 E Bellvue Pl; mains $5-10; 🕐 breakfast & lunch; Ⓜ Red Line to Clark/Division

Carb up on pancakes at this lovingly low-key option in the heart of the Gold Coast; made from scratch and piled in enormous stacks, they contend for the best breakfast in the city. If you're soaking up some of the excesses of the night before, order the 'Dutch Baby,' a formidable golden basket of doughy goodness.

🍴 PJ CLARKE'S *American* $$
☎ 312-664-1650; 1204 N State St; mains $8-23; Ⓜ Red Line to Clark/Division

Chicago's straight 30-somethings make for this pub to eyeball one another. Classy and cozy, PJ Clarke's specializes in comfort foods with high-end twists, such as the béarnaise burger and teriyaki skirt steak sandwich.

🍴 PUMP ROOM *American* $$
☎ 312-266-0360; www.pumproom.com; 1301 N State St, Ambassador East; mains $11-38; Ⓜ Red Line to Clark/Division

A classic on the Gold Coast strip, the Pump Room specializes in hair-straightening martinis and old school elegance. Real VIPs, or just lucky poseurs, sit in the dining room's legendary Booth One, a see-and-be-seen throwback to the glamorous days of the 1940s. The dress code insures you'll be well attired for the cheek-to-cheek dancing that begins most nights after dinner. Go for the delicate small plates unless you want to take on hearty mains such as the unctuous porterhouse or bison tenderloin.

🍴 SIGNATURE ROOM AT THE 95TH *American* $$$

☎ 312-787-9596; John Hancock Center, 875 N Michigan Ave; mains $12-39; Ⓜ Red Line to Chicago

Compared with the mind-blowing views that stretch out for miles, the menu of moderately fancy American surf and turf is capably executed, but not all that memorable. The lunch buffet ($14, served Monday to Saturday) is the best deal for the view, since the price of lunch is comparable to a foodless ticket to the observation deck. Families come for Sunday brunch; cheapskates get the same soul-stirring views for the price of a (costly) beer, one flight up in the Signature Lounge.

🍸 DRINK

🍸 GIBSON'S *Bar*

☎ 312-266-8999; 1028 N Rush St; 🕐 11am-1am; Ⓜ Red Line to Clark/Division

Gibson martinis (served with a cocktail onion) are the namesake item at this lively bar attached

---

GOODBYE, CABRINI-GREEN

Plagued by violent crime and bleak urban dysfunction, the Cabrini-Green housing projects would have likely made Chicago civic designer Daniel Burnham turn over in his grave. The towering red high-rise buildings were nationally notorious ghettos. But eventually the economic forces of the city surrounded the ghetto with affluent neighborhoods, and the 70-acre site caught the eye of real-estate developers. In 1996 the Chicago Housing Authority unveiled the Near North Redevelopment Initiative, which called for knocking down the crumbling towers and putting up mixed-income housing. The new plan incorporated homes for 2000 people in an area that formerly housed 15,000. Lawsuits alleged that the city had too hastily escorted out its former residents to slums further from the city center. Though the transformation of the neighborhood along Division St (between La Salle and Halsted Sts) is not yet complete, the name of Cabrini-Green has begun to disappear from city maps (mostly parceled up between Old Town and Lincoln Park), but it will likely take much longer to fade from people's memories. As for the quickie housing developments that are luring in luxury buyers? They might have made Burnham turn in his grave the other way.

to Gibson's steak house. See the review on p64 for details on sitting down to a slab of meat. A piano player starts up at 5pm.

🍸 LODGE *Bar*
☎ 312-642-4406; 21 W Division St; 🕐 5pm-4am Sun-Fri, to 5am Sat; Ⓜ Red Line to Clark/Division

Dressed up like a misplaced hunting cabin, the Lodge has a bit more polish than most of its neighbors on Division St. A Wurlitzer jukebox spins oldies, and the bowls of salty peanuts complement the abundant beers on tap. The crowd of mostly 40-somethings drink like they mean business.

⭐ PLAY

⭐ BACK ROOM *Nightclub*
☎ 312-751-2433; www.backroom chicago.com; 1007 N Rush St; Ⓜ Red Line to Clark/Division

This venerated Gold Coast jazz room is so cozy that there isn't a bad view in the house, even when you take in the stage via a long mirror. If the small main floor gets too tight, head up the spiral staircase and take things in from above. Bop purists be warned: the tunes here can get more than a little smooth.

⭐ COQ D'OR *Piano Bar*
☎ 312-787-2200; Drake Hotel, 140 E Walton St; 🕐 11am-2am Mon-Sat, to 1am Sun; Ⓜ Red Line to Chicago

With scores of tall-backed, wood-paneled hideaway booths and a tinkle of Cole Porter from the piano man, this subterranean bar is a low-key, secretive treat. Live music gets going nightly at 7pm.

⭐ ENCLAVE *Nightclub*
☎ 312-654-0234; www.enclavechicago .com; 220 W Chicago Ave; 🕐 9pm-2am Thu-Fri, to 3am Sat; 🚍 66

This newcomer to Chicago's club network is big – 15,000 sq ft of former warehouse redone with glossy hardwood floors and lively art installations. Even with the platform dancers and coy martini menu, it's fairly classy, bringing in Chicago celebs and a downtown crowd that dances to mainstream pan-genre hits.

⭐ LE PASSAGE *Nightclub*
☎ 312-255-0022; www.lepassage.com; 937 N Rush St; 🕐 7pm-4am Wed-Fri, to 5am Sat; Ⓜ Red Line to Chicago

Though it suffers a bit of a split personality – what with a faux-French name and a menu that includes a fruity concoction called a 'Scorpion Bowl' – this is a beautiful club with French-colonial decor. It makes the appropriate backdrop for would-be models and their pursuers, who mostly admire each other's cheekbones until the Polynesian libations wreak havoc and the dancing begins.

⭐ LEG ROOM *Nightclub*
☎ 312-337-2583; www.legroomchicago
.com; 7 W Division St; ☾ 9pm-4am
Mon-Wed, 7pm-4am Thu-Fri, to 5am Sat;
Ⓜ Red Line to Grand

The Leg Room might be a little
cheesy, with its wall-to-wall
crushed velvet, tired trance music
and shiny-faced singles, but the
laid-back vibe and friendly staff
make it the most inviting place to
gawk at the Rush St pick-up scene.

⭐ LOOKINGGLASS THEATRE
COMPANY *Theater*
☎ 312-337-0665; www.lookingglass
theatre.org; 821 N Michigan Ave; Ⓜ Red
Line to Chicago

This ensemble cast – which just
so happens to include cofounder
David Schwimmer of *Friends* – adds
physical stunts and spectacular
visuals to its vivid black box productions. The collaborative art
direction tends toward classic
stories such as *Brothers Karamazov,
Our Town* and *Arabian Nights*.

⭐ OAK STREET BEACH *Beach*
☾ dusk-dawn; Ⓜ Red Line to
Clark/Division

There aren't many cities outside
of Florida that offer so much sand
and (miniaturized) surf this close
to their major business districts.
Oak St Beach is a quaint spot,
a bit lower key than beaches
further north, where you're likely
to get a volleyball spiked on your
head. Try the 'Beachstro', which
offers a chance to escape the
sun's heat and cool off with a
delicious, mountainous ice-cream
sundae.

⭐ ZEBRA LOUNGE *Piano Bar*
☎ 312-642-5140; 1220 N State St;
☾ 2pm-2am Sun-Thu, to 3am Fri & Sat;
Ⓜ Red Line to Clark/Division

The piano can get as scratchy as
the voices of the crowd, which
consists mainly of older folks who
like to sing along. Regular ivory-
stroker Tom Oman is a veteran
who knows his stuff.

>LINCOLN PARK & OLD TOWN

As moms with Bugaboo strollers roll by on their way to fetch a skim latte, and graduated bobos bounce along making baby talk to their pugadoodles, it might seem as though Lincoln Park has plunged into the lowest circle of yuppie hell. But while Lincoln Park's upper-middle class invasion has certainly changed the tenor of the streets surrounding DePaul University, the area has undeniable charms. Great restaurants and boutiques, a sprawling oasis of ponds and paths, and the city's impeccable free zoo top the list. North Ave Beach washes up the south side of the 'hood, and further south and east is Old Town, the epicenter of Chicago's hippie culture in the 1960s. Visitors won't find too much in the way of sights, but Old Town outranks its more lively neighbors when it comes to comedy – improv bastion Second City is here.

LINCOLN PARK & OLD TOWN

👁 SEE
Chicago History
  Museum 1 G5
Lincoln Park
  Conservatory 2 F2
Lincoln Park Zoo 3 F3
St Valentine's Day
  Massacre Site 4 F3

🏠 SHOP
Dave's Records 5 E1
Spice House 6 F5
Uncle Dan's 7 D2
Vosges
  Haut-Chocolat 8 D4

🍴 EAT
Adobo Grill 9 F5
Alinea 10 D5
Cafe Ba-Ba-Reeba! 11 D3
Charlie Trotter's 12 D3
Merlo Restaurante 13 D1
Pequod's Pizza 14 B3
Trotter's To Go 15 C2
Twin Anchors 16 F5
Wiener's Circle 17 E1

🍸 DRINK
Deja Vu 18 D1
Delilah's 19 C1
Goose Island
  Brewery 20 D4

Kelly's 21 D3
Olde Town Ale House ..22 F5
Sterch's 23 E3

⭐ PLAY
B.L.U.E.S. 24 D2
Crobar 25 D5
Kingston Mines 26 D2
Lincoln Park 27 G4
North Ave Beach 28 H4
Second City 29 F5
Steppenwolf Theater ..30 D5

Please see over for map

👁 SEE

📷 CHICAGO HISTORY MUSEUM

☎ 312-642-4600; www.chicagohs.org; 1601 N Clark St; adult/12-18yr $12/10, Mon admission free; 🕒 9:30am-4:30pm Mon-Wed, Fri & Sat, to 8pm Thu, noon-5pm Sun; Ⓜ Brown or Purple Line to Sedgwick

By including troubling and triumphant chapters in the city's history, the gracefully remodeled Chicago History Museum is the best single stop for people curious about the city's storied past. Vivid multimedia displays cover the Great Fire and 1968 Democratic Convention, and detail local inventions that include the skyscraper, the nuclear reactor and the birth control pill. It also houses one of the city's best photo opportunities: the chance to dress up in the costume of a Chicago hot dog.

📷 LINCOLN PARK CONSERVATORY

☎ 312-742-7736; 2391 N Stockton Dr; admission free; 🕒 9am-5pm; 🚌 151

The glass conservatory features 3 acres of lush gardens and hosts a rotating array of annual flower shows. The Alfred Caldwell Lily Pool, immediately northeast of the conservatory, resembles the stratified canyons of the nearby Wisconsin Dells and has become a stopover for migrating birds.

📷 LINCOLN PARK ZOO

☎ 312-742-2000; www.lpzoo.com; 2200 N Cannon Dr; admission free; 🕒 10am-4:30pm Nov-Mar, to 5pm Apr-Oct, 10am-6:30pm Sat & Sun Jun-Aug; 🚌 151

The free zoo is one of Chicago's most popular attractions and its naturalistic Regenstein African Journey is the attraction at its finest. The Cat House and Primate House are musts, and the Farm-in-the-Zoo will delight young ones. If you come during colder months, you'll have many of the exhibits to yourself. See p17 for more.

ST VALENTINE'S DAY MASSACRE

Though crime in Lincoln Park these days is pretty much relegated to shoppers sneaking nuts from the bulk-food bins at Whole Foods, blood ran in the streets on February 14, 1929. That day, men dressed as cops showed up at a garage at 2122 N Clark St and gunned down six fellows working for Bugs Moran, a North Side Irish gang leader, who was trying to inch into the booze-running operation of Al Capone. The murders, which came to be known as the St Valentine's Day Massacre, were never pinned on Capone, who was vacationing in Florida at the time, but he did eventually get pinched for tax evasion and sent to Alcatraz.

SHOP

DAVE'S RECORDS
Record Shop

☎ 773-929-6325; www.davesrecords chicago.com; 2604 N Clark St; Ⓜ Brown or Purple Line to Diversey

With a splatter of colored vinyl decorating the back wall, Dave's feels a little like the setting of Nick Hornby's music-nerd classic, *High Fidelity*. CDs? Forget it. MP3s? Never heard of 'em. Dave's doesn't discriminate with genres, but it's for vinyl purists only.

SPICE HOUSE *Spice Shop*

☎ 312-274-0378; www.thespicehouse .com; 1512 N Wells St; 🕑 10am-7pm Mon-Sat, to 5pm Sun; Ⓜ Brown or Purple Line to Sedgwick

A bombardment of peppery fragrance socks you in the nose at this exotic spice house, offering delicacies such as black and red volcanic salt from Hawaii and pomegranate molasses among the tidy jars. Best though are the house-made herb blends themed after Chicago neighborhoods, including the piquant 'Argyle St Asian Blend,' allowing you to take home a taste of the city.

UNCLE DAN'S *Outdoor Gear*

☎ 773-477-1918; 2440 N Lincoln Ave; Ⓜ Red, Brown or Purple Line to Fullerton

This store offers top travel and outdoor gear for those looking to escape the concrete jungle, or at least get some abrasion-reinforced fleece to protect them from the elements. It's a relaxed place to buy gear, without the macho scoping of prowling sales dudes.

VOSGES HAUT-CHOCOLAT
Food & Drink

☎ 773-296-9866; 951 W Armitage Ave; Ⓜ Brown or Purple Line to Armitage

Owner-chocolatier Katrina Markoff's truffles have a national rep for bringing in exotic flavors such as curry, chili and wasabi. She even goes upscale with the simple candy bar: the heaven-sent dark chocolate blends are dressed up with sea salt, 'enchanted mushrooms' and bacon. Yes, bacon.

EAT

ADOBO GRILL *Mexican* $$

☎ 312-266-7999; 1610 N Wells St; mains $10-19; 🕑 closed lunch Mon-Fri; Ⓜ Brown Line to Sedgwick

Chef Paul LoDuca takes Mexican food and flavors to another dimension at his lively eatery near Second City. Yummy guacamole is made tableside, and the menu standouts include trout steamed in corn husks and tender chicken breasts in Oaxacan black mole sauce. Adobo also has over 80 sipping tequilas on hand to quench your thirst.

🍴 ALINEA *Contemporary* $$$
☎ 312-867-0110; www.alinea-restaurant.com; 1723 N Halsted St; prix-fixe menus $135-195; 🕑 dinner, closed Mon & Tue; Ⓜ Red Line to North/Clybourn
Superstar chef and James Beard Foundation Award winner Grant Achatz is in charge of the small dining room at Alinea. Among Chicago's most exhilarating spaces for foodies, Alinea's artistic carnival of food is served in steel and glass contraptions, created especially for each dish. Expect otherworldly single-bite dishes and futuristic delights, such as duck served with a 'pillow of lavender air.' A once-in-a-lifetime meal at this restaurant can take upwards of four hours.

🍴 CAFE BA-BA-REEBA!
Tapas $$
☎ 773-935-5000; www.cafebabareeba.com; 2024 N Halsted St; mains $12-30; Ⓜ Brown or Purple Line to Armitage
At this delightful tapas joint, the garlic-laced sauces may have you surreptitiously licking the plates. The menu changes daily but always includes some spicy meats, marinated fish and the city's most renowned small plates. For a main event, order one of the nine paellas ($12 per person) as soon as you

get seated – they take a while to prepare.

🍴 CHARLIE TROTTER'S
Contemporary $$$
☎ 773-248-6228; www.charlietrotters.com; 816 W Armitage Ave; prix-fixe menus $135 & $155; 🕑 closed Sun & Mon; Ⓜ Brown or Purple Line to Armitage; Ⓥ
Not unlike the mayoral monarchy, Charlie Trotter hasn't let go of his throne as king of Chicago's culinary world for many years, often making the short list of best fine dining experiences in the world. His eponymous restaurant presents seasonal ingredients with dead-serious preparation (his formidable rules prohibit staff from laughing in the kitchen). One of the three daily multicourse prix-fixe meals is a vegetable menu. Reservations are essential and often required at least four weeks in advance. Jackets required. For a less expensive taste of Trotter's artistry, try **Trotter's To Go** (☎ 773-868-6510; 1337 West Fullerton Ave), a deli-style store with succulent spit-roasted meats and the best fancy picnic fare in the Midwest.

🍴 MERLO RESTAURANTE
Italian $$$
☎ 773-529-0747; 2638 N Lincoln Ave; mains $16-39; 🚌 9 to Ashland & Webster
Bolognese regional fare is the forte of this cozy family-operated

slow-food bistro and wine bar, where steaming dishes of risotto-of-the-day and hand-rolled pastas dominate the menu, offering particular comfort when the weather turns cold.

🍴 PEQUOD'S PIZZA *Pizza* $

☎ 731-327-1512; 2207 N Clybourn Ave; mains $7-10; 🚌 9 to Ashland & Webster

Like the ship in *Moby Dick*, from which this neighborhood restaurant takes its name, Pequod's deep-dish is the thing of legend. It's head and shoulders above chain competitors because of its caramelized cheese, generous toppings and sweetly flavored sauce.

🍴 TWIN ANCHORS
American $$

☎ 312-266-1616; 1655 N Sedgwick St; mains $8-18; Ⓜ Brown Line to Sedgwick

Chicagoans speak of the Twin Anchors' baby-back ribs, with their smoky, tangy sauce, in agitated hyperbole. This spot doesn't take reservations, so you'll have to wait outside or around the neon-lit 1950s bar, which sets the tone. Sinatra on the jukebox completes the '50s supper-club ambience.

🍴 WIENER'S CIRCLE
American $

☎ 773-477-7444; 2622 N Clark St; mains $3-6; 🕐 24hr; Ⓜ Brown or Red Line to Diversey

PIGGING OUT: MORNING, NOON & NIGHT

In the last several years, Chicago has reclaimed its heritage as the nation's capital of edible oink, offering pork variations far beyond the famous hot dog. From a savory breakfast heart-stopper, to haute presentations of Euro schnitzel, this is a city that knows what to do with a pig.

> Breakfast: **Sweet Maple Cafe** (p128) – begin Chicago's 'tour d'swine' with an 'Egg & Cheesier' and sweet country sausage breakfast sandwich, sided with bone-in ham.
> Lunch: **Borinquen Restaurant** (p115) – spiced with garlic and cumin and served on fried plantain slices, the *jibarito* is a brilliant presentation of Puerto Rican pork.
> Snack: **Wan Shi Da Bakery** (p137) – one of the best places in Chinatown for smoky, tangy *char siu bao* (BBQ pork bun).
> Dinner: **Publican** (p127) – the entire menu at this buzzworthy West Loop location is dedicated to high class plates of pig.
> Dessert: **Vosges Haut-Chocolat** (p72) – Mo's Bacon Bar combines two great indulgences: savory bacon and decadently dark chocolate.
> Midnight Snack: **El Taco Veloz** (p105) – tacos piled high with sweet, succulent *el pastor* (fried pork).
> Take Home: **Spice House** (p72) – the 'Pullman Pork Chop Spice' will bring a taste of Chicago pork home.

Both infamous and revered in Chicago, Wiener's Circle's charred hot dogs come with a verbal berating that would make a sailor blush – it's not recommended for those with delicate feelings. Open 24/7, and popular when the bars have shut up shop, this Lincoln Park equivalent of a roadhouse usually reaches its frenetic peak around 4:30am.

DRINK

DEJA VU *Bar*
☎ 773-871-0205; 2624 N Lincoln Ave; ⏰ 9pm-4am Sun-Fri, to 5am Sat; Ⓜ Brown or Red Line to Fullerton
Open until 5am (!) on Saturdays, Deja offers more than just a deliriously late last call. The decor is a mix of opulent Middle Eastern and garage-sale art deco, with live bands or DJs and free pool thrown in.

DELILAH'S *Bar*
☎ 773-472-2771; 2771 N Lincoln Ave; ⏰ 4pm-2am Sun-Fri, to 3am Sat; Ⓜ Brown Line to Diversey
A bartender rightfully referred to this bad-ass black sheep of the neighborhood as the 'pride of Lincoln Ave,' a title earned by its underground rockers and best whiskey selection in the city. Among the discerning roster of single malts is one of its own making: Delilah's 13th Anniversary

Single Malt Scotch. If the 1st floor gets too rowdy, take things upstairs where it's a bit more sedate.

GOOSE ISLAND BREWERY *Brewery*
☎ 773-915-0071; 1800 N Clybourn Ave; ⏰ 11am-1am Mon-Fri, to 2am Sat, to midnight Sun; Ⓜ Red Line to North/Clybourn
Though its production swelled in recent years, the quality of hoppy handcrafted ales from this local brewery hasn't suffered. Honker's Ale and potent XXX Porter are fresher here than any taps around town. The patio opens up for its seasonal summer brew.

KELLY'S *Bar*
☎ 773-281-0656; 949 W Webster Ave; ⏰ 11am-2am Sun-Fri, to 3am Sat; Ⓜ Brown or Red Line to Fullerton
DePaul students, alumni and fans of DePaul's Blue Demons can get elbow to elbow at this classic pub that's been family owned and operated since the day after Prohibition ended. It's directly under the El, so hold onto your glass when a train goes by.

OLDE TOWN ALE HOUSE *Pub*
☎ 312-944-7020; www.oldtownalehouse.net; 219 W North Ave; ⏰ noon-4am Sun-Fri, to 5am Sat; Ⓜ Brown Line to Sedgwick

Cluttered with raunchy paintings (including a new notable one of 2008 vice president would-be Sarah Palin…nude), this Old Town staple has classic jazz on the juke-box and a jovial crowd.

☠ STERCH'S *Bar*
☎ 773-281-2653; 2238 N Lincoln Ave; ☽ 3:30pm-2am Sun-Fri, to 3am Sat; Ⓜ Brown or Red Line to Fullerton

'No Corona. No foolish drinks. Lim-ited dancing,' reads the sign in the window at this otherwise convivial dive. Those rules invite a genial older crowd of writers and grizzled neighborhood types, as does a jukebox stocked with Coltrane and the Stones.

⭐ PLAY

☆ B.L.U.E.S. *Blues Bar*
☎ 773-528-1012; www.chicagoblues bar.com; 2519 N Halsted St; Ⓜ Brown Line to Diversey

This narrow dive sends you home with ears ringing from high-volume blues. Big local names, such as Big James & the Chicago Playboys, crowd onto the small stage.

☆ CROBAR *Blues Bar*
☎ 312-266-1900; www.crobar.com; 1543 N Kingsbury St; ☽ 10pm-4am Wed & Fri, to 5am Sat; Ⓜ Red Line to North/Clybourn

This club harkens back to Chica-go's hedonistic past: the industrial space is enlivened by pastel high-lights and mirrors. High-minded techno rules the dance floor with a mixed crowd that is hipper, younger and here to party hard.

☆ KINGSTON MINES *Blues Club*
☎ 773-477-4646; www.kingstonmines .com; 2548 N Halsted St; Ⓜ Brown Line to Diversey

Popular enough to draw big names, it's so hot and sweaty here that blues neophytes will feel like they're having a genuine experi-ence – sort of like a gritty theme park. Two stages ensure lots of action.

☆ LINCOLN PARK *Park*
🚌 151

This park's 1200 acres stretch for 6 long miles, containing lakes and trails that offer plenty of op-portunities to get some fresh air regardless of the season. A visit demands a few minutes' repose before Augustus Saint-Gaudens' *Standing Lincoln*, a powerful image of the 16th president. (The artist also sculpted *Sitting Lincoln*, which rests its rump by the Art Institute.) From a dock in front of **Café Brauer**, a 1908 Prairie School architectural creation, you can rent two-person paddleboats and cruise the South Pond. The rental season is roughly May through September.

NEIGHBORHOODS

LINCOLN PARK & OLD TOWN

⭐ NORTH AVENUE BEACH
Beach

🕐 **dawn-dusk;** 🚌 **151**

One of the only Chicago locations to exude a southern California vibe, this sandy spot is strung with volleyball nets and skimpily dressed sunbathers. Dodgeball teams and roller-hockey leagues collide in beachside rinks and the steamship-inspired beach house contains a seasonal café. A short walk on the curving breakwater any time of year yields postcard city views.

⭐ SECOND CITY *Comedy Club*

☎ **312-337-3992; www.secondcity .com; 1616 N Wells St;** Ⓜ **Brown Line to Sedgwick**

A Chicago must-see, this club is symbolized by John Belushi, who emerged from the suburbs in 1970 with a creative, manic, no-holds-barred style. Belushi soon moved to the main stage, and then to *Saturday Night Live*. Second City's shows are sharp and biting commentaries on life, politics, love and anything else that falls in the crosshairs of their hard-hitting wit. **Second City Etc** houses a training company that often presents more risky work, as actors try to get noticed and make the main stage. Both theaters offer the city's best comedy value after the last show most nights, when the comics present free improv performances.

⭐ STEPPENWOLF THEATER
Theater

☎ **312-335-1650; www.steppenwolf .org; 1650 N Halsted St;** Ⓜ **Red Line to North/Clybourn**

With 20,000 annual subscribers and productions of the highest quality, this legendary name in Chicago theater was founded by Terry Kinney, Gary Sinise and Jeff Perry. It quickly outgrew one space after another, won a Tony in 1985 for regional theater excellence, and is a leading international destination for dramatic arts. Among the many famous alumni are John Malkovich, Gary Cole and John Mahoney.

Lincoln Park's landmark stage, Steppenwolf

>LAKE VIEW & WRIGLEYVILLE

Of all the interesting cultural collisions in Chicago, few are as divergent as those around Lake View and Wrigleyville, where mobs of chest-bumping, beer-swilling, Cubs-cheering revelers party a few blocks away from the rainbow banners of Boystown, the gay district that centers on N Halsted St between Belmont Ave and Addison St. The cluster of bars and restaurants lining Clark St and Southport Ave go for an impish dose of carousing by night. Belmont, just west of Boystown, is the youngest of Lake View's pockets, and the stores cater to the lifestyle whims of goths, punks and kitschy hipsters. For all its copious energy, Lake View has little in the way of historic sights or cultural attractions beyond the ballpark. Just bring your credit cards, walking shoes and festive attitude, and you'll be set. When the Cubs are in town, avoid the place like the plague if you dislike crowds.

LAKE VIEW & WRIGLEYVILLE

● SEE
Alta Vista Tce 1 E3
Chicago Cubs ....(see 2)
Wrigley Field 2 E3

🏠 SHOP
A Okay Official 3 F5
Alley 4 F5
Architectural Artifacts ..5 C1
Army Navy Surplus
    USA 6 D5
Chicago Comics 7 F5
Fourth World Artisans ..8 D3
Gay Mart 9 F4
Gramaphone Records ..10 G6
Strange Cargo 11 E4
Uncle Fun 12 D5
Yesterday 13 E4

🍴 EAT
Chicago Diner 14 F4
Clark St Dog 15 F5
Crisp 16 G6
HB 17 F4
Mia Francesca 18 F4
Platiyo ....(see 18)
Tango Sur 19 D3
Victory's Banner 20 B4
Yoshi's Cafe 21 F5

🍸 DRINK
Closet 22 G4
Cubby Bear 23 E4
Duke of Perth 24 G6
Gentry 25 F4
Ginger Man 26 E3

Guthrie's 27 D3
Hungry Brain 28 A5
Murphy's Bleachers 29 F3
Ten Cat Tavern 30 D2
Yak-zies 31 E3

⭐ PLAY
Beat Kitchen 32 B5
Berlin 33 F5
Circuit 34 F3
ComedySportz 35 F6
IO (ImprovOlympic) 36 E4
Metro 37 E3
Schubas 38 D5

Please see over for map

👁 SEE

👁 ALTA VISTA TERRACE

btwn Byron & Grace Sts; Ⓜ Red Line to Sheridan

Chicago's first designated historic district is worthy of the honor. Developer Samuel Eberly Gross re-created a block of London row houses on Alta Vista Tce in 1904. The 20 exquisitely detailed homes on either side of the street mirror each other diagonally, and the owners have worked hard at maintaining the spirit of the block.

👁 BOYSTOWN

btwn Halsted & Broadway Sts, Belmont Ave & Addison St; Ⓜ Red Line to Addison

Flags flying proudly in Boystown

Boystown is one of the biggest Lesbian Gay Bisexual Transgender (LGBT) communities in the country. The streets of Boystown are full of rainbow flags and packed with bars, shops and restaurants. For more info on gay Chicago, see the boxed text, p149.

👁 WRIGLEY FIELD

☎ 773-404-2827; 1060 W Addison St; Ⓜ Red Line to Addison

Behind the statue of departed announcer Harry Caray lies the woefully unlucky Cubbies' home, the second-oldest ball park in the major leagues. For information about the park and obtaining tickets, see p16. If you don't get tickets, check out the 'knothole' or head to the corner of Kenmore and Waveland Aves, where ball hawks wait to snag errant home runs that fly over the wall.

🛍 SHOP

🛍 A OKAY OFFICIAL
Sportswear

☎ 773-248-4547; www.aokayofficial .com; 3270 N Clark St; Ⓜ Red, Brown or Purple Line to Belmont

Local artists design and customize sneakers, which are sold alongside skate decks, prints and playful bling. It's a hip, urban space where sneakerheads clamor for crazy, rare, limited-edition kicks (typically costing upward of $100).

Map labels

Columns: A B C D

Rows: 1 2 3 4 5 6

W Montrose Ave

Montrose Ⓜ

N Ravenswood Ave

5

N Hermitage Ave

N Paulina St

W Cullom Ave

See Andersonville, Lincoln Square & Uptown Map p93

W Berteau Ave

N Ashland Ave

W Belle Plaine Ave

Irving Park Ⓜ

W Irving Park Rd

30

W Byron St

N Hermitage Ave

N Paulina St

N Marshfield Ave

W Grace St

19

N Western Ave

8

W Waveland Ave

N Southport Ave

N Damen Ave

Addison Ⓜ

W Addison St

2

N Lincoln Ave

Kinko's

W Cornelia Ave

20

W Roscoe St

Paulina Ⓜ

Southport Ⓜ

W Henderson St

W School St

W Melrose St

N Southport Ave

12

W Belmont Ave

32

38

W Fletcher

28

W Belmont Ave

N Ashland Ave

N Greenview Ave

W Barry Av

See Logan Square & Humboldt Park Map p113

6

N Lincoln Ave

N Paulina St

W Nelson St

W Wellington Ave

W Oakdale Ave

North Branch Chicago River

W George St

W Wolfram St

W Diversey Ave

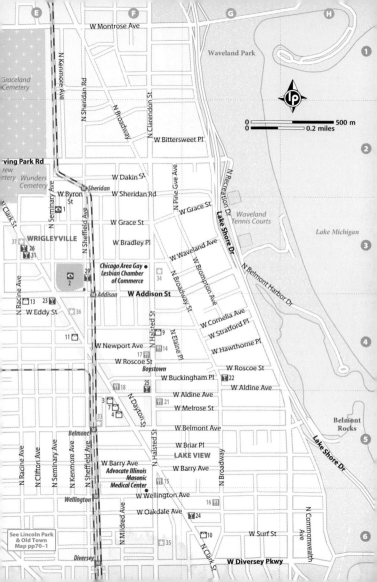

E | F | G | H

W Montrose Ave

Waveland Park

1

N Kenmore Ave
N Sheridan Rd
N Broadway

Graceland
Cemetery

W Bittersweet Pl

N Clarendon St

500 m

0.2 miles

2

ving Park Rd

rew
nery   Wunders
Cemetery

W Dakin St

N Pine Gve Ave

N Clark St

N Seminary Ave

W Byron
St

Sheridan

W Sheridan Rd

W Byron St

N Recreation Dr

Waveland
Tennis Courts

Lake Michigan

1

N Sheffield Ave

W Grace St

W Grace St

Lake Shore Dr

WRIGLEYVILLE

W Bradley Pl

N Belmont Harbor Dr

3

37

26
31

W Waveland Ave

N Brompton Ave

N Racine Ave

Chicago Area Gay
Lesbian Chamber
of Commerce

29

2

34

W Addison St

Addison

W Cornelia Ave

4

13   23

W Eddy St

36

N Halsted St

9

N Elaine Pl

W Stratford Pl

W Hawthorne Pl

11

W Newport Ave

17

14

Belmont
Rocks

W Roscoe St

W Roscoe St

Boystown

18

25

W Buckingham Pl

22

W Aldine Ave

5

3

7

33

4

N Dayton St

21

W Aldine Ave

W Melrose St

Belmont

W Belmont Ave

LAKE VIEW

W Briar Pl

N Racine Ave
N Clifton Ave
N Seminary Ave
N Kenmore Ave
N Sheffield Ave

W Barry Ave

W Barry Ave

N Broadway

Advocate Illinois
Masonic
Medical Center

15

Wellington

W Wellington Ave

16

6

W Oakdale Ave

24

See Lincoln Park
& Old Town
Map pp70–1

N Mildred Ave

10

W Surf St

35

N Commonwealth Ave

Diversey

N Clark St

W Diversey Pkwy

Lake Shore Dr

🏠 ALLEY *Clothing & Accessories*
☎ 773-525-3180; www.thealley.com;
3228 N Clark St; Ⓜ Red, Brown or Purple
Line to Belmont

Skull and crossbones mark the door at this one-stop counter-culture shop. The Alley offers pot pipes, leathers and human-sized dog collars. Loud, obnoxious punk-rock T-shirts and punk leathers are a speciality of the house.

🏠 ARCHITECTURAL ARTIFACTS *Antiques*
☎ 773-348-0622; www.architecturalartifacts.com; 4325 N Ravenswood Ave;
Ⓜ Brown Line to Montrose

This mammoth 80,000-sq-ft warehouse, a bit northwest of Lake View proper, is a treasure trove of Italian marionettes, 1920s French mannequins and Argentinean cast-iron mailboxes. Be sure to step into the free, attached Museum of Historic Chicago Architecture, with works by all the big names in Chicago architecture, including Louis H Sullivan and Frank Lloyd Wright.

🏠 ARMY NAVY SURPLUS USA *Clothing, Outdoor Gear*
☎ 773-348-8930; www.armynavysales.com; 3100 N Lincoln Ave; Ⓜ Brown Line to Southport

Sure, it's kind of a mess, but among the torn boxes and shambles of merchandise there are some cool old military surplus items. (Who knows when you'll need a parachute?)

🏠 CHICAGO COMICS *Comics*
☎ 773-528-1983; www.chicagocomics.com; 3244 N Clark St; Ⓜ Red, Brown or Purple Line to Belmont

This comic emporium has won the 'best comic book store in the US' honor and its shelves are shared by Marvel *Superman* back issues and cutting-edge local artists, such as Chris Ware, Ivan Brunetti and Dan Clowes.

🏠 FOURTH WORLD ARTISANS *Arts & Crafts*
☎ 773-404-5200; www.fourthworldartisans.com; 3727 N Southport Ave;
Ⓜ Brown Line to Southport

Handmade dolls, bowls and brightly patterned local crafts and musical instruments, arriving from as far as Vietnam, Ghana and Pakistan, and as near as Chicago's immigrant enclaves, fill this bazaar.

🏠 GAY MART *Adult Toyshop*
☎ 773-929-4272; www.gaymart.com; 3457 N Halsted St; Ⓜ Red Line to Addison

A general store for gay and lesbian novelties, clothes, toys and books. One of the top sellers is Billy, the heroically endowed 'world's first out and proud gay doll.' Poor Ken would wilt in Billy's presence.

Make your own souvenir Chicago T-shirt at one-of-a-kind Strange Cargo

GRAMAPHONE RECORDS
Music Store

☎ 773-472-3683; www.gramaphone
records.com; 2843 N Clark St; Ⓜ Brown
or Purple Line to Diversey

With vinyl plates of rare electro,
techno and hip-hop, Gramaphone
is one of the hippest record stores
in Chicago. Along with its collection of trendsetting sounds to take
home, Gramaphone has info on
upcoming parties.

STRANGE CARGO
Clothing & Accessories

☎ 773-327-8090; www.strangecargo
.com; 3448 N Clark St; Ⓜ Red Line to
Addison

Check out Strange Cargo for
stylish vintage gear, iron-ons and
hipster wear; it also sells wigs,
clunky shoes and leather jackets.
Buy a vintage-style pattern – say,
one of the Picasso sculpture – then
use the iron-on machine to enli-
ven it with a message or decal of
your choice. There's an excellent
selection of kitschy ones featuring
Ditka (see p87), the city flag and
the Hancock Centre, all supreme
souvenirs.

UNCLE FUN *Toyshop*

☎ 773-477-8223; www.unclefunchica
go.com; 1338 W Belmont Ave; ☯ closed
Mon; Ⓜ Red, Brown or Purple Line to
Belmont

NEIGHBORHOODS

LAKE VIEW & WRIGLEYVILLE

The mission at this whimsical novelty shop is f-u-n, and it's one of the best spots in Chicago for fun gifts, kitschy postcards and vintage games. The shelves are overflowing with tin robots, fake mustaches and the 'Mess o' Maligned Mammals.'

🎁 YESTERDAY Toyshop
☎ 773-248-8087; 1143 W Addison St; Ⓜ Red Line to Addison

Historic sports and movie memorabilia are the specialities at this nostalgic shop, where books, posters and thousands of old baseball cards are jammed into a single-story building that predates some of the historical items for sale.

🍴 EAT
🍴 CHICAGO DINER
Vegetarian $
☎ 773-935-6696; 3411 N Halsted St; mains $5-11; Ⓜ Red Line to Belmont; Ⓥ

The gold standard for Chicago vegetarians, this place has been serving barbecue seitan (a meat substitute), wheatmeat and tofu stroganoff for over 20 years. The hip staff is friendly, and will guide you to the best stuff on the menu, including the peanut butter vegan 'supershakes' and 'Radical Ruben,' a lunch plate that earns its popularity.

🍴 CLARK STREET DOG
American $
☎ 773-281-6690; 3040 N Clark St; mains $5-10; 🕐 9am-3am Sun-Thu, to 4am Fri & Sat; Ⓜ Red Line to Chicago

Clark Dog is the brighter, friendlier version of the brash Weiner's Circle (p74), with only a smidgeon of the confrontational attitude. Apart from hot dogs, other carnivorous delights include the hearty combo – which marries Italian beef and Italian sausage on a single soggy bun – and the chili cheese fries. If all the salty dogs make you thirsty, head to the supremely divey adjoining Clark Street Bar for some cheap cold ones.

🍴 CRISP
Korean $
☎ 877-693-8653; www.crisponline.com; 2940 N Broadway; mains $6-12; 🕐 11.30am-9pm Tue-Thu & Sun, to 10.30pm Fri & Sat; Ⓜ Red Line to Belmont

At this cheerful café, hits pour out of the stereo and amazingly cheap, delicious Korean fusions are delivered fresh from the kitchen. The 'Bad Boy Buddha' bowl, a variation on *bi bim bop* (mixed vegetables with rice), is the best $7 lunch in town. Or, on second thoughts, maybe that award goes to Crisp's burrito, filled with perfectly fried chicken in a savory soy ginger sauce.

HB *New American* $$
☎ 773-661-0299; 3404 N Halsted St;
mains $8-14; ✖ closed lunch Tue-Fri,
closed Mon; Ⓜ Brown, Purple or Red
Line to Belmont

The monogram stands for 'Home
Bistro,' where careful comfort food
is served in a warm wood-and-tile-
lined space. On the weekend, chef-
owner Joncarl Lachman serves a
justly famous brunch, while exquisite pork chops and pan-fried crabs
rule the dinner menu. BYOB.

MIA FRANCESCA *Italian* $$
☎ 773-281-3310; 3311 N Clark St;
mains $10-25; Ⓜ Brown or Red Line to
Belmont

Diners quickly fill up the dining
room at one of the most popular
family-run Italian bistros in the
city. The frequently changing
handwritten menu features earthy
standards with aggressive season-
ing from southern Italy. Other
treats include wafer-thin pizzas
and the often-overlooked staple of
Italian kitchens, polenta.

PLATIYO *Mexican* $$
☎ 773-477-6700; 3313 N Clark St; mains
$9-18; Ⓜ Brown or Red Line to Belmont

The warm dining room of this
creative Mexican restaurant is
packed with locals who come for
the upbeat atmosphere and haute
dishes, such as mahi-mahi tacos

A vegetarian's haven – Chicago Diner. Fancy a peanut butter supershake?

and zingy shrimp fajitas. The chef of Platiyo learned his chops working at the unmatched Frontera Grill (p54), and you can taste the mastery – at least until you've imbibed too many items from the inventive margarita menu.

🍴 TANGO SUR
Argentine Steak House $$
☎ 773-477-5466; 3763 N Southport Ave; mains $11-27; 🕑 closed lunch Mon-Sat; 🚌 80

This candlelit BYOB steak house makes an idyllic date, serving classic skirt steaks and other tender grass-fed cuts. The chef's special is 'Bife Vesuvio,' a prime strip stuffed with garlic, spinach and cheese – it's a triumph. In summer, outside tables expand the seating of the small, spare interior.

🍴 VICTORY'S BANNER
Vegetarian, Brunch $
☎ 733-665-0227; www.victorysbanner.com; 2100 W Roscoe St; mains $6-9; 🅼 Brown Line to Paulina; 🆅

The tough decision at this revered breakfast house is between the fresh, free-range egg omelets and the legendary French toast, cooked in rich cream batter and sided with peach butter. New Age tunes and muted colors give it a soothing vibe, even when the place is mobbed on weekend mornings.

🍴 YOSHI'S CAFE *Japanese* $$
☎ 773-248-6160; 3257 N Halsted St; mains $16-26; 🕑 closed Mon; 🅼 Brown or Red Line to Diversey; 🆅

Yoshi and Nobuko Katsumura preside over one of the most innovative casual places in town, with a menu focused on healthy dishes with a Japanese flair. The kitchen treats all ingredients with the utmost respect, from the salmon to the tofu in the vegetarian dishes.

🍸 DRINK

🍸 CLOSET *Bar*
☎ 773-477-8533; 3325 N Broadway St; 🕑 2pm-4am Mon-Fri, noon-5am Sat, to 4am Sun; 🅼 Brown or Red Line to Belmont

One of the very few lesbian-centric bars in Chicago, the Closet changes mood and tempo at 2am, when the crowd becomes more mixed, the music gets louder and things get a little rowdier.

🍸 DUKE OF PERTH *Pub*
☎ 773-477-1741; 2913 N Clark St; 🕑 5:30pm-2am Mon, 11:30am-2am Tue-Fri, to 3am Sat, noon-2am Sun; 🚌 22

The UK beers and 80-plus bottles of single-malt scotch are nearly overwhelming at this cozy, laid-back pub. After enough of them, try the fish and chips, which is all-you-can-eat for lunch and dinner for $9 on Wednesday and Friday.

Y GENTRY *Bar*
☎ 773-348-1053; 3320 N Halsted St; ◷ 4pm-2am Sun-Fri, to 3am Sat; Ⓜ Brown or Red Line to Belmont
This stately, brick-walled piano bar serves as a welcome respite for 30- and 40-year-old gay men, weary of the pounding house beats of Boystown's clubs. Live cabaret music nightly.

Y GINGER MAN *Bar*
☎ 773-549-2050; 3740 N Clark St; ◷ 3pm-2am Mon-Fri, noon-3am Sat, to 2am Sun; Ⓜ Brown or Red Line to Diversey
A splendid place to pass an evening, Ginger Man features a huge, eclectic beer selection, along with reprieve from the Cubs mania by playing classical music and jazz during home games. Come here for free pool on Sundays.

CHICAGO SPORTS ICONS 101

If you don't know your Ditka from your Butkus, here's a survival manual for macho small talk in Chicago taverns.

Bobby Hull (aka the Golden Jet) The Blackhawks left winger is considered one of hockey's all-time greats.

Dick Butkus (aka Dick Butkus) Elected to the Pro Football Hall of Fame in 1979, the Bears player recovered 25 fumbles in his career, a record at the time of his retirement.

Ernie Banks (aka Mr Cub) Voted the National League's most valuable player (MVP) twice (1958 and 1959), he was the first baseball player to have his number retired by the Cubs.

Michael Jordan (aka Air Jordan) Bulls hero who ended his career of 15 seasons with the highest per-game scoring average in NBA history.

Mike Ditka (aka Iron Mike) The Chicago Bears former coach (and current Chicago restaurateur), and the only person to have won a Super Bowl as a player, assistant coach and head coach. And what a mustache!

Ozzie Guillen (aka Ozzie) Current White Sox coach and former player, known for his outspoken and politically incorrect comments. He brought the World Series trophy to Chicago in 2005 – the first big win in almost 100 years.

Ryne Sandberg (aka Rino) The Cubs second baseman played a record 123 consecutive games without an error, and in 2005 became the fourth Cubs player ever to have his number retired.

Walter Payton (aka Sweetness) The Chicago Bears great is ranked second on the National Football League (NFL) all-time rushing list, and seventh in all-time scoring.

Elia Einhorn
Singer, songwriter and leader of Scotland Yard Gospel Choir, a rock band on Chicago indie label Blood Shot Records; waiter at Chicago Diner

What's different about Chicago's music scene? Chicago's big enough to have an amazing and varied music scene, but small enough that you know almost everyone in it, including (quote-unquote) rock stars. You'll see Wilco out seeing other bands and you can have a beer with them. Or a Shirley Temple. **Why is there so much music here?** It's so much cheaper than New York or LA. You'll see labels like Thrill Jockey, which began in New York and moved here. Labels can have big warehouses here and bands can actually literally practice in the garage. Musicians can afford to live. **Best-sounding room in town** Schubas (p91). It's a fan's room. **Iconic music room** The Metro (p91). You know that Dylan, Morrissey and any of your heroes have played there. **Best place to get an instant feel for the scene** The Hideout (p110) and Empty Bottle (p110). The Hideout is a place where people who have gone on to become famous got their start. **Favorite scene figurehead** Cynthia Plaster Caster. When Belle and Sebastian were in town last time, I took them to meet her at the Hideout, and the New Pornographers were hanging out. That's Chicago; it couldn't happen anywhere else.

GUTHRIE'S *Bar*
☎ 773-477-2900; 1300 W Addison St; ◷ 4pm-2am; Ⓜ Red Line to Addison
A local institution, Guthrie's remains pretty mellow even as the neighborhood goes ballistic around it. The glassed-in back porch is fittingly furnished with patio chairs and filled with 30- and 40-somethings, with most tables sporting a box of Trivial Pursuit cards. European soccer and rugby fanatics are also dedicated patrons, rewarded when the bar occasionally opens at 6am to show games live via satellite.

HUNGRY BRAIN
Bar, Jazz Club
☎ 773-935-2118; 2319 W Belmont Ave; ◷ 7pm-4am Sun-Fri, to 5am Sat; 🚌 77
The kind bartenders, roving tamale vendors and well-worn charm are inviting at this Roscoe Village staple, which hosts sets of free live jazz from some of the city's best young players on Sunday nights.

MURPHY'S BLEACHERS
Sports Bar
☎ 773-281-5356; 3655 N Sheffield Ave; Ⓜ Brown or Red Line to Diversey
Getting well lubricated before the big game is the prerogative of Cubs fans at this well-loved, historic watering hole, only steps away from the entrance to Wrig-

ley's bleacher seats. They jam this place like sardines on game day.

TEN CAT TAVERN *Pub*
☎ 773-935-5377; 3931 N Ashland Ave; ◷ 3pm-2am Sun-Fri, to 3am Sat; 🚌 9
Pool is serious business on the two vintage tables that Ten Cat Tavern co-owner Richard Vonachen refelts regularly with material from Belgium. The ever-changing, eye-catching art comes courtesy of neighborhood artists. Regulars (most in their 30s) down leisurely drinks at the bar or, in warm weather, head to the beer garden.

YAK-ZIES *Sports Bar*
☎ 773-525-9200; 3710 N Clark St; ◷ 11am-4am Sun-Fri, to 5am Sat; Ⓜ Brown or Red Line to Diversey
The covered outdoor patio and reasonable prices make Yak-zies the best place in Wrigleyville to cheer on the Cubs. Many a greasy high-five has been exchanged over heaping piles of chicken wings and Tang Chicken Pizza (a buffalo chicken covered pie). To enter the eye of the hurricane, head down the block and elbow into the famous **Cubby Bear** (☎ 773-327-1662; 1059 W Addison St; ◷ call for opening hours; Ⓜ Red or Brown Line to Diversey), where the beer can be expensive and the whooping fraternity reunion gets downright unruly.

⭐ PLAY

⭐ BEAT KITCHEN *Live Rock Club*

☎ 773-281-4444; www.beatkitchen
.com; 2100 W Belmont Ave; 🚌 72
Everything you need to know is in
the name – entertaining, eclectic
beats and better-than-average
dinners. Music in the homely back
room can be funky or jammy, but
a crop of Chicago's smart, broadly
appealing songwriters dominates
the calendar.

⭐ BERLIN *Dance Club*

☎ 773-348-4975; www.berlinchicago
.com; 954 W Belmont Ave; 🕒 8pm-4am
Mon & Sun, 5pm-4am Tue-Fri, 5pm-5am
Sat; Ⓜ Brown or Red Line to Belmont
Stepping off the El at Belmont
has long been one of the city's
best bets for finding a packed,
sweaty dance floor. Berlin caters
to a mostly gay crowd during
the week, though partyers of all
sexual proclivities jam the place
on the weekends. Whatever the
day, monitors flicker through the
latest videos from cult pop and
electronic performers, while DJs
take the dance floor on trancey
detours.

⭐ CIRCUIT *Dance Club*

☎ 773-325-2233; www.circuitclub.com;
3641 N Halsted St; 🕒 9pm-4am Thu, Fri,
Sun & Mon, to 5am Sat; Ⓜ Red Line to
Addison

The classiest of the Boystown
nightclub mainstays has a lovely
rooftop deck where a highly styl-
ized, sexually mixed crowd whiles
away the summer evenings. It's
also the perfect perch for looking
down their noses at the mobs of
shirtless twinks at the club next
door, Hydrate. Don't leave without
trying the fat-free alcoholic slush-
ies or visiting the Star Trek room.

⭐ COMEDYSPORTZ
Improv Comedy

☎ 773-549-8080; www.comedysportz
chicago.com; 2851 N Halsted St; Ⓜ Red
or Brown Line to Diversey
The gimmick? Two improv teams
compete with deadly seriousness
to make you laugh hysterically. The
audience benefits from this comic
capitalism, and all the fun is G-
rated. Alcohol is allowed, but BYOB.

⭐ IO (IMPROVOLYMPIC)
Improv Comedy

☎ 773-880-0199; www.improvolympic
.com; 3541 N Clark St; Ⓜ Red Line to
Addison
The Olympic Committee forced this
comic veteran to change the name
to its initials in 2005, a suitably
laughable development in a long
career of chuckles. ImprovOlympic
launched the careers of Mike Myers
and MTV's Andy Dick, along with a
host of other well-known comics.
Shows hinge entirely on audience

suggestions, and each turn can run 40 minutes or longer. If you're thoroughly motivated by what you see, IO offers a range of courses to suit every budget.

⭐ METRO *Live Music Theater*
☎ 773-549-0203; www.metrochicago.com; 3730 N Clark St; Ⓜ Red Line to Addison

Acts teetering on the verge of superstardom play this former classic theater, which has the sight lines and sound system to make it among the best venues in Chicago.

⭐ SCHUBAS *Live Music Club*
☎ 773-525-2508; www.schubas.com; 3159 N Southport Ave; Ⓜ Brown or Red Line to Belmont

Something of an alt-country legend, Schubas presents a host of twangy, acoustic artists and indie rock acts that don't get booked across town at the Empty Bottle (p110). While the bar area itself is friendly and boisterous, the music room out the back is for serious listening only – chatty patrons should expect to be shushed.

>ANDERSONVILLE, LINCOLN SQUARE & UPTOWN

You can smell it in the air: this northern neighborhood demonstrates how the sprawling fabric of modern Chicago was first stitched together by immigrant communities surrounding downtown. There's butter-scented air wafting over Swedish bakeries in Andersonville, the starchy smelling beer halls of the former German enclave Uptown, and the turmeric that lingers over Argyle St, named 'Little Saigon' for the glut of Vietnamese eateries that shot up in recent years. Predictably, history seeps from the streets here, a part of town where jazz houses imported gangland booze during Prohibition and movie lots turned out silent flicks starring Charlie Chaplin and WC Fields. And, of course, there's plenty of evidence of the newest of newcomers to the neighborhood in the upscale baby boutiques and fancy-pants foodie joints.

Andersonville, Lincoln Sq and Uptown may be a bit of a hike from the city center, but a quick El ride brings you to destinations exuding a quiet European charm that feels aeons away from the racket of the Loop.

ANDERSONVILLE, LINCOLN SQUARE & UPTOWN

👁 SEE

⊙ ARGYLE STREET

**btwn Broadway Ave & Sheridan Rd;
Ⓜ Red Line to Argyle**

Rounding the corner from Broadway Ave onto Argyle St, everything is suddenly decked out in Laotian, Vietnamese and Cambodian script. Many of the area's residents came here as refugees from the Vietnam War, filling the storefronts with lunch spots and great window-shopping opportunities. Besides, who doesn't get the occasional hankering for a fertilized duck egg?

⊙ HUTCHINSON STREET DISTRICT

Ⓜ Red Line to Sheridan

In contrast to some of Uptown's seedier areas, the Hutchinson St District is a proud, well-maintained enclave of homes built in the early 1900s, representing some of the best examples of Prairie School residences in Chicago. Several, such as number 839, are the work of George W Maher, a famous student of Frank Lloyd Wright.

⊙ SWEDISH AMERICAN MUSEUM CENTER

☎ 773-728-8111; www.samac.org; 5211 N Clark St; adult/child $4/3; ⊙ 10am-4pm Tue-Fri, 11am-4pm Sat & Sun; Ⓜ Red Line to Berwyn

Land, ho! Swedish American Museum Center

The permanent collection at this tidy storefront museum focuses on the Swedish immigrants who settled here, with butter churns, traditional furniture and religious relics.

🛍 SHOP

⌂ ALAMO SHOES *Shoes*

☎ 773-784-8936; www.alamoshoes.com; 5321 N Clark St; Ⓜ Red Line to Berwyn

This throwback to the 1960s focuses on comfortable Swedish shoes and Birkenstocks for both men and women, all at really good prices. The enthusiastic staffers hop off to the back room and emerge with stacks of boxes until you find what you want or you're entirely walled in by the possibilities.

🍫 BON BON *Food & Drink*
☎ 773-784-9882; www.bonbonchicago.com; 5110 N Clark St; 🕐 closed Mon & Tue; Ⓜ Red Line to Berwyn

A mother-daughter team infuses handmade chocolates with exotic, heady ingredients such as rose petals, chilies and chai. As if it wasn't sensuous enough, the pieces are then molded into figures from the Kama Sutra (as well as King Tut and other figurines – which, in context, are still kind of sexy).

🍫 EARLY TO BED *Sex & Fetish*
🕐 773-271-1219; www.early2bed.com; 5232 N Sheridan Rd; 🕐 closed Mon; Ⓜ Red Line to Berwyn

This low-key, women-owned sex shop is friendly to novices, providing explanatory pages and customer reviews to help discern butt beads from bullet vibes. Also on hand are feather boas, bondage tapes and vegan condoms (made free of a milk-derived product usually used in latex production).

📚 WOMEN & CHILDREN FIRST *Bookstore*
☎ 773-769-9299; www.womenandchildrenfirst.com; 5233 N Clark St; Ⓜ Red Line to Berwyn

High-profile book-signings (including Hillary Clinton) and author events happen weekly at this welcoming shop, which features fiction and nonfiction by and about women.

🍴 EAT

🍴 ANN SATHER *American* $
☎ 773-271-6677; www.annsather.com; 5207 N Clark St; mains $6-13; Ⓜ Red Line to Berwyn

The cinnamon rolls are the marquee item at the flagship of this small, friendly local chain that offers Swedish standards in a pleasant cafe environment. Filling, familiar Nordic offerings, such as meatballs and potato sausages, join delicious selections of American comfort food on the dinner menu.

🍴 HAI YEN *Vietnamese, Chinese* $$
☎ 773-989-0712; 1007 W Argyle St; mains $5-25; 🕐 closed Wed; Ⓜ Red Line to Argyle

Many of the dishes at this warm Argyle St eatery require some assembly, pairing shrimp with rice crepes, mint, Thai basil and lettuce. The *bo bay mon* consists of seven (yes, seven) different cuts of beef. Order sparingly, or ask for some help from your server – many of the dishes are large enough to feed an army.

BUTTERING UP IN ANDERSONVILLE

Suck it in! This neighborhood is going to be rough on your girlish figure; the food up here is *killer*. Fatten up with these tempting treats, close enough to each other that you'll roll from one mind-blowing taste to another without burning any of it off:

> Marzipan-filled artisan pastries at Pasticceria Natalina (below)
> Buttery Swedish baked goods from Ann Sather (p95)
> Sticky coconut rice with mango at Thai Pastry (opposite)
> Kama Sutra curried chocolate at Bon Bon (p95)
> Ale-soaked mussels and *frites* and a goblet of Belgian beer at Hopleaf (p98)

🍴 JIN JU *Korean* $$
☎ 773-334-6377; 5203 N Clark St; mains $7-17; 🕒 dinner; Ⓜ Red Line to Berwyn

The candlelit interior of Jin Ju is minimalist and echoes softly with downbeat techno, while stylish 30-somethings enjoy 'nouveau Korean' mains, such as *haemul pajon* (a fried pancake stuffed with seafood) and *kalbi* (beef short ribs).

🍴 LEONARDO'S RESTAURANT *Italian* $$
☎ 773-561-5028; 5657 N Clark St; mains $8-25; 🕒 closed Mon; Ⓜ Red Line to Berwyn

A quaint atmosphere and delicious traditional Tuscan fare make this a fiercely guarded local neighborhood favorite. No yawnish pasta and meatballs here: the 18-hour ravioli – stuffed with a mouth-watering combination of braised osso buco and goat cheese, and covered in caramelized pearl onions, sage and a

succulent demi glaze – is the champion of the menu.

🍴 M HENRY *Brunch* $$
☎ 773-561-1600; www.mhenry.net; 5707 N Clark St; mains $8-10; 🕒 breakfast & lunch; Ⓜ Red Line to Berwyn

A contender for best brunch in the city, the wait is worth it at M Henry, which nails both savory and sweet brunch items on a seasonal menu.

🍴 PASTICCERIA NATALINA *Italian Bakery* $
☎ 773-989-0662; www.p-natalina.com; 5406 N Clark St; mains $5-8; 🕒 7am-6pm Tue-Fri, 8am-5pm Sat & Sun; Ⓜ Red Line to Berwyn

The friendly little bakery of Natalie and Nick Zarzour achieves the most authentic, lovingly made Italian sweets in the city by importing ingredients and recipes from the motherland. The creations change daily, and most watchful visitors pick up some *cassata,* an Italian liqueur-soaked cake filled with sweet ricotta cream and covered in marzipan and candied fruit.

⊞ THAI PASTRY *Thai* $

☎ 773-784-5399; www.thaipastry.com; 4925 N Broadway; mains $5-10; Ⓜ Red Line to Argyle

A lunchtime favorite with workers from both Uptown and Andersonville, this Thai restaurant has a window filled with awards, and the food to back it up. The spot-on curries arrive still simmering in a clay pot. For a quick, cheap snack, visit the counter for a baked pastry.

🍸 DRINK

🍸 BIG CHICKS *Bar*

☎ 773-728-5511; 5024 N Sheridan Rd; 🕐 4pm-2am Mon-Fri, to 3am Sat, 3pm-2am Sun; Ⓜ Red Line to Argyle

Uptown's Big Chicks has an enjoyable bipolar disorder: during the week the bar is a cozily sedate place for gay and straight people to socialize beneath the sizable collection of woman-themed art, while on weekends gay men pack the stamp-sized dance floor and boogie until the wee hours. There's also a legendary free barbecue brunch every Sunday at Big Chicks.

Patrons enjoying one of the best beer bars in town, Hopleaf (p98)

HOPLEAF *Gastro-Pub*

☎ 773-334-9851; www.hopleaf.com; 5148 N Clark St; ⏰ 3pm-2am Mon-Fri & Sun, to 3am Sat; Ⓜ Red Line to Berwyn

Using the name of the national beer from his ancestral Malta, Hopleaf owner Michael Roper operates one of the city's best and classiest beer bars. The overwhelming selection of beers is artfully chosen by Roper, with an emphasis on Belgian and American brews. The kitchen serves excellent Belgian *frites* and mussels.

★ PLAY

★ BLACK ENSEMBLE THEATER *Theater*

☎ 773-769-4451; www.black ensembletheater.org; Uptown Center Hull House, 4520 N Beacon St; Ⓜ Red Line to Wilson

This well-established group saw their fledgling production of *The Jackie Wilson Story* attract wide attention and national tours. The focus here has long been on original productions about the African American experience,

A classic, candlelit Chicago jazz club, Green Mill

CHAPLIN, CHICAGO & THE SILVER SCREEN

He never uttered the words on screen, but Charlie Chaplin captured Chicago's character ably in his 1964 book *My Autobiography*, speaking about the city that was, for a short while, his home. 'It had a fierce pioneer gaiety that enlivened the senses,' he wrote. 'Yet underlying it throbbed masculine loneliness.' Anyone who has laughed at Chaplin's famous silent character, The Tramp, knows the same words could be used to describe the comic genius himself. In the days before sound revolutionized cinema, long before Hollywood was, well, *Hollywood*, Chaplin lived and worked in Chicago, which produced more movies than any other city in the US at the time. Chaplin worked at the leader of Chicago's movie houses, Essanay, which turned out some 2000 silent films with other household names such as Gloria Swanson, WC Fields and Gilbert M Anderson. Among Chaplin's dozen Essanay comedies are his celebrated *The Tramp* (filmed in Essanay's West Coast studios), *By the Sea*, *The Bank* and *In the Park*. Chaplin eventually split with Essanay over creative differences and the company folded in 1917, about the time that much of its roster was being lured to the bright lights of a still-nascent Hollywood. You can wander past the building that housed the studio at 1345 W Argyle St, now part of St Augustine's College (which has a hall named after the actor). The pair of terra-cotta Indian heads that faces the Essanay logo are an aptly quiet reminder of the epicenter of the city's influence during the silent film era.

through mostly biographical, historic scripts.

⭐ GREEN MILL *Jazz Club*
☎ 773-878-5552; www.greenmilljazz
.com; 4802 N Broadway; Ⓜ Brown Line
to Lawrence
You can sit in Al Capone's favorite spot at the timeless Green Mill, Chicago's oldest nightclub, a true cocktail lounge that comes complete with curved leather booths and colorful tales about mob henchmen who owned shares in the place. Little has changed in

70 years – the club still books top local and national jazz acts.

⭐ NEO-FUTURISTS *Comedy Theater*
☎ 773-275-5255; www.neofuturists
.org; 5153 N Ashland Ave; Ⓜ Red Line
to Berwyn
Best known for its long-running, brilliant *Too Much Light Makes the Baby Go Blind,* in which the hyper troupe makes a manic attempt to perform 30 plays in 60 minutes. Admission cost is based on a dice throw.

>WICKER PARK, BUCKTOWN & UKRAINIAN VILLAGE

If you want to get a taste of artsy young Chicago, wander up Milwaukee Ave near Damen Ave in Wicker Park on a Friday night. Pass booming bars, packed restaurants and stages hosting indie rock on one side of the street and shushed underground author readings on the other. By Saturday morning, patrons browse dozens of cool boutiques, bookstores, restaurants and salons. Buttressed by the slightly fancier Bucktown and slightly scruffier Ukrainian Village, there is *a lot* happening in this neighborhood, so strap on some comfortable (hip) sneakers and take it block by block.

Although signs of the neighborhood's past are fading fast, there are plenty of traces of the Eastern European immigrants who founded it, especially in the western reaches of Ukrainian Village. A stroll here will take you past Ukrainian scrawl on shop windows, Orthodox churches and proud, if humble, corner taverns where immigrants have long quenched their thirst.

WICKER PARK, BUCKTOWN & UKRAINIAN VILLAGE

Please see over for map

◉ SEE

◉ NELSON ALGREN HOUSE

1958 W Evergreen Ave; Ⓜ Blue Line to Damen

In this apartment building, writer Nelson Algren created some of his greatest works about the gritty Chicago of yesteryear. Algren won the 1950 National Book Award for his *The Man with the Golden Arm*. You can't go into the house, but you can admire it from the street.

◉ UKRAINIAN INSTITUTE OF MODERN ART

☎ 773-227-5522; www.uima-chicago .org; 2320 W Chicago Ave; admission free; ☼ noon-4pm Wed-Sun; 🚌 66

The 'Ukrainian' in the name is somewhat of a misnomer, as this bright white storefront showcases local artists of all ethnicities. The space has earned a reputation for playful and proactive multimedia exhibits.

🛍 SHOP

🛍 BORING STORE *Toyshop*

☎ 773-772-8108; 1331 N Milwaukee Ave; Ⓜ Blue Line to Damen

Operated by literacy-focused nonprofit group 826CHI, this zany spy-gear supplier has mustache kits, underwater voice amplifiers and banana-shaped cases to hide your cell phone in. Best of all, the sneaky stuff profits after-school

---

NELSON ALGREN & THE 'CITY ON THE MAKE'

Though Chicago has numerous literary lights, few shine with such defiant, blinding intensity as Nelson Algren, longtime Wicker Park resident and author of *Chicago: City on the Make*, *The Man with the Golden Arm* and *A Walk on the Wild Side*. Advice from the last of these captures Algren's acrid sense of humor – 'Never play cards with a man called Doc. Never eat at a place called Mom's. Never sleep with a woman whose troubles are worse than your own' – but the first of these is his essential must-read on the city's character, short enough to be read on the plane ride into town. In 2009 Algren's 100th birthday brought a series of quiet celebrations to the neighborhood. While in Wicker Park, stroll through the remnants of Algren's Chicago.

Lottie's Pub (☎ 773-489-3250; www.lottiespub.com; 1925 W Cortland St; Ⓜ Blue Line to Damen) Today it's just a sports bar, but its sordid history of gambling, gangsters, strippers and prostitutes made it Algren's favorite.

Myopic Books (p104) This superlative used bookstore is the center of the neighborhood's literary world, a great place to stock up on Algren, hear live music and spend a rainy afternoon.

Nelson Algren Fountain (cnr Milwaukee & Ashland Aves & Division St) This redesigned fountain stands near Chicago's Polish Triangle, a part of town that inspired many of his works.

Nelson Algren House (above) You can't go in, but Algren's 3rd-floor apartment is a top destination for literary visitors.

writing and tutoring programs that take place on-site.

HABIT *Clothing & Accessories*
☎ 773-342-0093; 1951 W Division St; ☽ closed Mon; Ⓜ Blue Line to Division

There's little gear for nuns in this space devoted to 15 indie, mostly local designers. With a showcase of simple-but-chic dresses and purses, the look is upscale, and prices are relatively affordable. Relatively. Many pieces cost around $100.

MYOPIC BOOKS *Bookstore*
☎ 773-862-4882; www.myopicbook store.com; 1564 N Milwaukee Ave; ☽ 11am-1pm Mon-Sat, to 10pm Sun; Ⓜ Blue Line to Damen

Sunlight pours through the windows of the city's oldest and largest used bookstore, which serves coffee and hosts poetry readings and experimental music. In other words, it's perfect.

PORTE ROUGE *Homewares*
☎ 773-269-2800; 1911 W Division St; Ⓜ Blue Line to Division

Behind the door of this French-kissed shop, aspiring gourmets get outfitted with hand-painted crockery, chic kitchen accessories and a wide selection of fine teas.

QUIMBY'S *Comics*
☎ 773-342-0910; 1854 W North Ave; Ⓜ Blue Line to Damen

See and be 'zine at Quimby's comic shop

The epicenter of Chicago's comic and 'zine worlds, Quimby's is one of the linchpins of underground culture in the city. You can find everything here from crayon-powered punk manifestos to slick graphic novels.

RECKLESS RECORDS
Record Store
☎ 773-235-3727; 1532 N Milwaukee Ave; Ⓜ Blue Line to Damen
Chicago's best indie-rock record and CD emporium allows you to listen to everything before you buy. This is the place to get your finger on the pulse of Chicago's au courant underground rock scene.

T-SHIRT DELI
Clothing & Accessories
☎ 773-276-6266; 1739 N Damen Ave; Ⓜ Blue Line to Damen
They take the 'deli' part seriously here: after they cook (aka iron a retro design on) your T-shirt, they wrap it in butcher paper and serve it with chips. Choose from heaps of styles and decals, from Mao and Patty Hearst to a giant bong.

🍴 EAT
ALLIANCE BAKERY *Bakery* $
☎ 773-278-0366; 1736 W Division St; mains $5-7; Ⓜ Blue Line to Division
This awesome independent bakery turns out great sandwiches (if you get lunch, a little dessert comes with your meal) and baked goods. In the large, comfy room next door, café patrons enjoy the goodies and free wireless.

COLD COMFORTS CAFÉ
Deli $
☎ 773-772-4552; 2211 W North Ave; mains $6-8; ⏲ 8am-4pm Tue-Sat, 9am-3pm Sun; Ⓜ Blue Line to Damen
Cold Comforts begrudgingly serves a ham and cheese to the unadventurous, but its menu is jammed with thrilling offerings such as 'Who Is Che Guevara?' or the 'Torta de Kosher Salchicha' (strips of kosher dogs, lettuce, tomato, mozzarella and chipotle sauce).

EL TACO VELOZ *Mexican* $
☎ 312-738-0363; 1745 W Chicago Ave; mains $4-11; ⏲ 7am-2am Mon-Thu, to 3:30am Fri & Sat; Ⓜ Blue Line to Chicago
After the bars close, the cheap Mexican platters and rhythm of (mostly) Latino karaoke make this place the ultimate last call.

FLO *Southwestern, Brunch* $$
☎ 312-243-0477; www.eatatflo.com; 1434 W Chicago Ave; ⏲ closed Mon; Ⓜ Blue Line to Chicago
The southwestern-bent dishes and first-rate brunch draw hordes of late-rising neighborhood hipsters on the weekend, though tart, potent *mojitos* and an elegant menu take over after dark.

🍴 GREEN ZEBRA
New American $$

☎ 312-243-7100; 1460 W Chicago Ave; mains $8-15; 🕐 dinner, closed Mon; 🚌 66; Ⓥ

With a few nods to carnivores, chef Shawn McClain's menu is mostly focused on amazing odes to seasonal, meatless meals, arty infusions (black-truffle essence, anyone?) and rich broths.

🍴 HOT CHOCOLATE *Dessert* $
☎ 773-489-1747; 1747 N Damen Ave; mains $7-19; 🕐 closed Mon; Ⓜ Blue Line to Damen

The Kobe beef skirt steak and mussels are good, but you could make a meal from the peerless sweets, care of renowned pastry chef Mindy Segal.

🍴 IRAZU *Costa Rican* $
☎ 773-252-5687; 1865 N Milwaukee Ave; mains $4-10; 🕐 closed Sun; Ⓜ Blue Line to Western

This hole-in-the-wall turns out Costa Rican burritos bursting with chicken, black beans and fresh avocado, and sandwiches dressed in a heavenly Costa Rican 'mystery sauce.' Try the oatmeal shake: it's like drinking an oatmeal cookie.

🍴 LE BOUCHON *French* $$
☎ 773-862-6600; 1958 N Damen Ave; mains $12-23; 🕐 dinner, closed Sun; Ⓜ Blue Line to Damen

With deep green tiles and crisp table linens, this romantic local bistro charms with a textbook lyonnaise salad and other note-perfect French fare, such as escargot and chocolate *marquisse* (chocolate mousse without the egg whites).

🍴 MARGIE'S *Ice Cream* $
☎ 773-384-1035; 1960 N Western Ave; mains $6-11; 🕐 9am-1am; Ⓜ Blue Line to Western

This brilliantly tattered ice-cream parlor on the outer northwest edge of Wicker Park has piled mountainous sundaes since 1921. The tables are few and a wait is common. But so, *so* worth it.

🍴 MILK & HONEY *American* $
☎ 773-395-9434; 1920 W Division St; mains $6-10; 🕐 lunch; Ⓜ Blue Line to Division

A bright, stylish space for an excellent breakfast or lunch, Milk & Honey fills with discerning Ukrainian Village socialites. Most of the dishes are prepared from scratch by co-owner Carol Watson (don't miss the mac 'n' cheese).

🍴 MIRAI SUSHI *Japanese* $$
☎ 773-862-8500; 2020 W Division St; mains $9-23; 🕐 dinner; Ⓜ Blue Line to Damen

This high-energy Japanese restaurant gets packed with happy, shiny Wicker Park residents enjoying fresh cuts of fish. With trance-hop electronic music and sleek staffers, Mirai is where connoisseurs of sashimi and *maki* (rolled sushi) throw back a few cocktails with their yellowtail and shiitake tempura.

🍴 PIECE *Pizza, Brewpub* $
☎ 773-772-4422; www.piecechicago.com; 1927 W North Ave; mains $6-12; ⏲ 11:30am-1:30am Mon-Thu, to 2am Fri, to 3am Sat; Ⓜ Blue Line to Damen
After hefting enough gooey bricks of deep-dish, the thin, flour-dusted crust of a 'New Haven-style' pizza at this spacious pizzeria and microbrewery offers a welcome reprieve. The best is the white variety – a sauceless pie dressed in olive oil, garlic and mozzarella. The easygoing, sky-lit ambience changes after dark, when ball games beam down from ubiquitous flat-screen TVs, and the 30-somethings get boisterous.

🍴 SPRING *New American* $$
☎ 773-395-7100; 2039 W North Ave; mains $15-28; ⏲ dinner, closed Mon; Ⓜ Blue Line to Damen
The seafood mains at this award-winning place have an Asian bent, as chef Shawn McClain dresses lobster, grouper and scallops with soy glazes, hot and sour broth, and fresh wasabi. The restaurant – a bathhouse in a former life – looks a little like an Ikea showroom, with simple, modern lines and muted greens.

🍴 UNDERDOG *American* $
☎ 773-772-1997; 1570 1/2 N Damen Ave; mains $1-7; Ⓜ Blue Line to Damen
This rowdy subterranean late-night hot-dog stop is a drunkard's paradise after a long night on Wicker Park bar stools.

🍴 VIENNA BEEF FACTORY STORE & DELI *American* $
☎ 773-235-6652; 2501 N Damen Ave; mains $3-6; ⏲ lunch, closed Sun; 🚌 50
After eating them all over town, it's worth a trip to the source. The Vienna Beef Factory makes the majority of hot dogs sold in Chicago, and the factory's deli serves the famous creations superfresh.

🍴 WEST TOWN TAVERN *New American* $$
☎ 312-666-6175; 1329 W Chicago Ave; mains $14-20; ⏲ dinner, closed Sun; 🚌 66
The exposed brick walls and tin ceiling warm the atmosphere, where carefully crafted and balanced American staples are refined enough to thrill, but still unpretentious enough to savor. The champion dish is its take on the humble pot roast, which falls apart with a buttery tenderness.

WICKER PARK, BUCKTOWN & UKRAINIAN VILLAGE

▼ DRINK

▼ CHARLESTON *Bar*

☎ 773-489-4757; 2076 N Hoyne Ave;
🕐 3pm-2am Mon-Sat, from noon Sun;
🚌 50

The resident cats curl up on your lap at this laid-back favorite of Bucktown locals. When the occasional folk and bluegrass acts set up in the middle of the narrow room, it gets crowded, but it's definitely worth it.

▼ DANNY'S *Bar*

☎ 773-489-6457; 1951 W Dickens Ave;
🕐 7pm-2am Sun-Fri, to 3am Sat; 🚌 50

Little Danny's is a hipster magnet, featuring a comfortably dim and dog-eared atmosphere and oc-

casional DJ sets of Stax 45s. Blessedly TV-free, it's a great place to come for conversation early in the evening, or to shake a tail feather at an impromptu dance party on the weekend.

▼ HAPPY VILLAGE *Bar*

☎ 773-486-1512; 1059 N Wolcott Ave;
🕐 4pm-2am Mon-Fri, to 3am Sat, noon-2am Sun; Ⓜ Blue Line to Damen

The sign boasting the 'happiest place in the east village' seems like an understatement. But on a summer evening when a strolling tamale vendor appears on the vine-covered patio – then it's the happiest place on Earth. Don't get sauced before entering the table-

Patrons cozy up in the snug atmosphere at Danny's

CHICAGO AT THE MOVIES

Although there's a 2004 film starring John Cusack that takes its name after Chicago's Wicker Park neighborhood, it is hardly the city's cinematic calling card – the remake of a French romantic thriller was described by a *New Yorker* film critic as 'remake hell.' But Chicago has been the backdrop for a number of classics (and cult classics).

> *The Sting* (1973) – a blockbuster cast including Robert Redford and Paul Newman tells the tale of confidence men and hustlers in Chicago's 1930s underbelly.
> *The Blues Brothers* (1980) – Chicago's comic golden boy John Belushi stars in this cult classic tale of two bluesmen on the run. Tons of great Chicago musicians cameo.
> *Ferris Bueller's Day Off* (1985) – the mischievous truant of this John Hughes classic visits Chicago highlights including the Art Institute (p37) and Wrigley Field (p79).
> *Candyman* (1992) – according to local legend, producers of this movie, the first in a trilogy of wonky slasher films set in the Cabrini-Green ghetto, had to strike a deal with gang members, filming them as extras in exchange for protection.
> *The Fugitive* (1993) – a growling Harrison Ford tries to right his name while being hunted by Tommy Lee Jones, who won an Academy Award for Best Supporting Actor for the role.
> *High Fidelity* (2000) – Chicagoan John Cusack stars in this tale about a snobby record-store clerk based on a novel of the same name by British author Nick Hornby.
> *The Dark Knight* (2008) – Chicago is the backdrop of this shadowy superhero tale that set records at the box office.

tennis room adjoining the bar: the competition is fierce.

☗ MATCHBOX *Bar*

☎ 312-666-9292; 770 N Milwaukee Ave; ⏱ 4pm-2am Mon-Fri, 3pm-3am Sat, 3pm-2am Sun; 🚌 56

Patrons jam this *extremely* cozy bar for some of the best (and most potent) cocktails in the city, made from scratch. Favorites include the Pisco Sour and ginger gimlet, ladled from a vat of homemade ginger-infused vodka. When the weather warms, claustrophobics take solace on the sidewalk patio.

☗ VIOLET HOUR *Bar*

☎ 773-252-1500; 1520 N Damen Ave; ⏱ 8pm-2am Sun-Fri, to 3am Sat; Ⓜ Blue Line to Damen

The unmarked, poster-covered edifice lends this newcomer the atmosphere of a highbrow speak-easy, matched by elaborately engineered cocktails (homemade bitters are applied with an eyedropper over six varieties of ice). Explore the menu of playfully haughty bar food by Justin Large, hot-handed owner of Avec (p125). If you have time for only one cocktail in the Windy City, order it here.

⭐ PLAY

⭐ DOUBLE DOOR Live Music
☎ 773-489-3160; www.doubledoor
.com; 1572 N Milwaukee Ave; Ⓜ Blue
Line to Damen

Just-under-the-radar alternative
rock finds a home at this former
liquor store, which still has its original sign and remains a landmark
around the Wicker Park bustle.

⭐ EMPTY BOTTLE Live Music
☎ 773-276-3600; www.emptybottle
.com; 1035 N Western Ave; Ⓜ Blue Line
to Damen

With its photo booth and parade of
Chicago's rock insiders, the Empty
Bottle gets its pick of the smaller
buzz bands to come through town.
The impressive programming here
doesn't stick to electric guitars and
power chords, however: free-jazz
master Ken Vandermark has been a
mainstay of the venue.

⭐ HIDEOUT Live Music
☎ 773-227-4433; www.hideoutchicago
.com; 1354 W Wabansia Ave; 🚌 72

Maybe it's all the Pabst, the industrial surroundings, or the room

Music fans propping up Empty Bottle's bar

of sweaty thrift-store-bedecked hipsters grinding to soul records at the postshow dance party, but this two-room lounge can be downright transcendent. On the weekend, the crowd goes every which way, and ultralate dance parties end the night. The outside of the building sports a mural of Barack Obama.

⭐ REDMOON THEATER
Puppetry

☎ 312-850-8440; www.redmoon.org; 1463 W Hubbard St; Ⓜ Green Line to Ashland

The interaction of humans and puppets is key to the magical, haunting adaptations of classic works such as *Moby Dick* and new commissions including *The Princess Club,* a fairly twisted look at children's fairy tales. The innovative nonprofit troupe is headed up by performance artists Blair Thomas and Jim Lasko and never fails to mesmerize.

⭐ SONOTHEQUE *Nightclub*

☎ 312-226-7600; 1444 W Chicago Ave; ⏰ 8pm-2am Wed-Fri, to 3am Sat; Ⓜ Blue Line to Chicago

The DJs here spin genres of electronic music that are so hip they don't even have names, but are perfectly matched with the futuristic space. Down-to-earth patrons and reasonable drink prices make it feel like the corner pub of 2015.

NEIGHBORHOODS

WICKER PARK, BUCKTOWN & UKRAINIAN VILLAGE

>LOGAN SQUARE & HUMBOLDT PARK

These neighborhoods, on the northwest edge of the city, feel far from the action, and their wide, quiet residential blocks and small corner shops are mostly untouched by tourist traffic. For now. Recently a new crop of young folks chased cheaper rents out here, settling around a small park, Logan Sq, and a larger one, Humboldt Park. Still mostly Latino, these neighborhoods are changing, and it seems like another new restaurant, bar or shop pops up every few months, especially around the increasingly bustling corner that faces the Logon Sq El stop. It's still a languid location that doesn't warrant exploring if you're on a short trip, but if you find yourself anywhere around here, do not miss the heart-stopping *jibarito* sandwich (garlic-mayo-slathered steak served between sliced-plantain 'bread'). If you're here on a sunny day, pack a couple of the savory sandwiches to go and hit the expansive Humboldt Park, which has plenty of quiet, grassy open space to lounge among the locals.

LOGAN SQUARE & HUMBOLDT PARK

◉ SEE
Boathouse **1** C5
Formal Garden **2** C6
Humboldt Park **3** C5
Illinois Centennial
 Memorial Column **4** C3
Puerto Rican Flag
 Sculpture **5** D6

⬛ SHOP
Wolfbait & B-girls **6** C3

🍴 EAT
Borinquen Restaurant .. **7** D5
Hot Doug's **8** D1
Kuma's Corner **9** C1
Lula Café ....(see 13)

▼ DRINK
Small Bar **10** C2
Whirlaway Lounge **11** C3

⭐ PLAY
Elastic Arts
 Foundation **12** B2
Logan Square
 Auditorium **13** C3
Rosa's Lounge **14** B4

NEIGHBORHOODS

LOGAN SQUARE & HUMBOLDT PARK

👁 SEE

🎯 HUMBOLDT PARK

1359 N Humboldt Blvd (also called N Sacramento Ave); 🚍 70

This 207-acre park, which lends its name to the surrounding neighborhood, is filled with a large iris- and brush-lined lagoon. The Prairie School boathouse rises up from the lagoon's edge as the park's showpiece, standing across the street from the riot of colorful flower beds and walk-through fountain of the Formal Garden. The park has gone through some rough times since German naturalist Alexander von Humboldt built it in 1869, but even though its revival in the past decade makes it family-filled by day, it's best avoided at night. The annual Fiestas Puertorriqueñas (Puerto Rican party) takes over the park in mid-June (see p24).

🎯 ILLINOIS CENTENNIAL MEMORIAL COLUMN

intersection of Kedzie Ave, Logan Blvd & Milwaukee Ave; Ⓜ Blue Line to Logan Sq

The towering phallic object standing in the middle of Logan Sq commemorates the 100th anniversary of Illinois' statehood. It was designed by Henry Bacon, the same architect who created the Lincoln Memorial in Washington DC. The reliefs of Native Americans, explorers, farmers and

CHICAGO RENT BY NEIGHBORHOOD

So, you're having such a good time that you want to move here? Here's a handy guide to Chicago rent by neighborhood. Prices are based on an average price for one-bedroom listings, for one month's rent.

> Andersonville: $890
> Bucktown: $925
> Gold Coast: $1725
> Humboldt Park: $750
> Lincoln Park: $1550
> The Loop and Near North: $1700
> Ukrainian Village: $1175
> Wrigleyville: $1125

laborers surrounding the base represent the great changes of the state's first century.

🎯 PASEO BORICUA

Division St btwn Western Ave & Mozart Ave; 🚍 70

Paseo Boricua, aka the Puerto Rican Passage, is a mile-long stretch of Division St stuffed with Puerto Rican shops and restaurants. It's marked at either end by a 45-ton, steel Puerto Rican flag sculpture that arches over the road; the eastern flag stands at Western Ave, while the western one is at Mozart Ave. This area has long been the epicenter of Chicago's 113,000-strong Puerto Rican community.

🛍 SHOP
🛍 WOLFBAIT & B-GIRLS
Arts & Crafts

☎ 312-698-8685; www.wolfbaitchicago
.com; 3131 W Logan Blvd; 🕙 closed Mon;
Ⓜ Blue Line to Logan Sq

Old ironing boards serve as display tables, while tape measures, scissors and other designers' tools hang from vintage hooks. You get that crafting feeling as soon as you walk in, and indeed, Wolfbait & B-girls both sells the wares (tops, dresses, handbags and jewelry) of local indie designers and serves as a working studio for them. You can even take a fabric printing workshop ($30, materials and drinks included, two hours).

🍴 EAT
🍴 BORINQUEN RESTAURANT
Puerto Rican $$

☎ 773-442-8001; www.borinquen
jibaro.com; 1720 N California Ave; mains
$6-20; Ⓜ Brown Line to Western

The story goes that Borinquen owner Juan 'Peter' Figueroa created his signature dish after reading an article in a Puerto Rican newspaper about a sandwich that subbed plantains for bread – a flash of inspiration that birthed the *jibarito*, an auspiciously popular dish that piles steak, lettuce,

Bring out your inner craftsperson at ubercool Wolfbait & B-girls

Doug Sohn
Owner of 'Sausage Superstore and Encased Meat Emporium,' Hot Doug's, Chicago native, begrudgingly faithful Cubs fan, first Chicago restaurateur to get fined for violating the city's short-lived 2006 ban on foie gras, which he used in a gourmet hot dog

On favorite Chicago foods One of the great things I've seen in the last 10 to 15 years is incredible growth in great restaurants and great cooks. Growing up you had a couple of steak houses; that was about it. Now, the city is defined by people such as Paul Kahan, who opened Blackbird (p126) and Publican (p127). Publican is one of the places you just can't stop eating because you haven't even heard of that kind of pork yet. I also love going down to Maxwell St (p135) to eat tacos at the Mexican food stands. The Hopleaf (p98) is another of my favorite restaurants; the beer selection and what they crank out of that tiny kitchen is amazing. **On the Chicago hot dog** It has a great rep, but there are very few doing it well. Most places cut corners to make it cheaper. The reason I'm still around is simple: we make a great Chicago hot dog.

tomato and garlic mayo between two thick, crisply fried plantain slices. It's the marquee item at Borinquen, though more traditional Puerto Rican fare is also available at the homey family spot.

🍴 HOT DOUG'S *American* $
☎ 773-279-9550; www.hotdougs.com; 3324 N California Ave; mains $2-5; 🕒 lunch, closed Sun; 🚌 77

The gourmet sausages served here by the owner, Doug, may be at the forefront of a Chicago hot-dog revolution. With specialities ranging from blueberry-merlot-venison to sesame-ginger-duck, the food at this friendly place has reviewers dragging out their superlatives. On Friday and Saturday, Doug offers fries cooked in thick duck fat (you have to ask for them).

🍴 KUMA'S CORNER
American $$
☎ 773-604-8769; www.kumascorner.com; 2900 W Belmont Ave; mains $10; 🕒 11:30am-2am Mon-Fri, 11:30am-3am Sat, 10am-11pm Sun; 🚌 77 to Elston

Kuma's is a dark corner of heaven, where a soundtrack of thrashing rock complements a roster of burgers themed after heavy-metal icons. The results can be straightforward (Black Sabbath comes blackened with chili and pepper

Hot diggedy Doug! Wrap your chops around a gourmet tail o' the pup at Hot Doug's

jack), esoteric (Led Zeppelin: pulled pork, bacon, cheddar and pickles) or whimsical (Judas Priest: bacon, blue cheese, fruit and nuts), and the concept has a cult following. Combative diners should try the Slayer, served sans-bun atop fries, with ingredients including 'anger.' Be warned: on winter days there's no outdoor seating, so the prime-time wait can be over two hours.

⅄ LULA CAFÉ *New American* $$
☎ 773-489-9554; www.lulacafe .com; 2573 N Kedzie Ave; mains $8-22; 🕒 closed Tue; Ⓜ Blue Line to Logan Sq; Ⓥ

The brunch at this friendly, upmarket café might be worth the trip out here alone. Even the muffins are something to drool over. And lunch? Watch out. Items include pasta *yiayia* (bucatini with Moroccan cinnamon, feta and garlic) and marinated rib eye with braised kale.

⅄ DRINK
⅄ SMALL BAR *Bar, Café*
☎ 773-509-9888; 2956 N Albany Ave; 🕒 4pm-2am Mon-Fri, 11am-3am Sat, 11am-2am Sun; Ⓜ Blue Line to Logan Sq

Its ace jukebox, affordable food and kindly staff make this unpretentious gem an easygoing place to spend an evening. The mirror behind the bar dates back to 1907.

⅄ WHIRLAWAY LOUNGE *Bar*
☎ 773-276-6809; 3224 W Fullerton Ave; 🕒 1pm-1:30am; Ⓜ Blue Line to Logan Sq

With threadbare couches and board games, this neighborhood fave has the homey charm of your uncle's '70s rumpus room – if your uncle had loads of hip pals with an insatiable thirst for Pabst. Sweetheart owner Maria Jaimes is saintly.

★ PLAY
☆ ELASTIC ARTS FOUNDATION
Performance Space
☎ 773-880-5402; www.elasticrevolu tion.com; 2830 N Milwaukee Ave, 2nd fl; Ⓜ Blue Line to Logan Sq

Lula Café: worth the trip for brunch

The calendar at Elastic Arts is far-reaching and impossible to pin down – one week the city's most exciting experimental choreo-graphers will fill the space, and the next will see a performance of original art music by cutting-edge international ensembles. Regardless, this is at the edge of Chicago's art community.

⭐ **LOGAN SQUARE AUDITORIUM** *Performance Space*
☎ 773-252-6179; www.lsachicago .com; 2539 N Kedzie Ave; Ⓜ Blue Line to Logan Sq

Logan Sq's legions of gentrifying scene-makers need some place to catch grimy, DIY, underground rock, and this spacious former ballroom answers the call. The gigs here, like the neighborhood, are a work in progress.

⭐ **ROSA'S LOUNGE** *Blues Bar*
☎ 773-342-0452; swww.rosaslounge .com; 3420 W Armitage Ave; 🚌 73
This is hard-core blues. Top local talents perform at this unadorned West Side club in a neighborhood that's still a few decades away from attracting developers. Take a cab.

>NEAR WEST SIDE & PILSEN

Although none of the neighborhoods in the Near West Side and Pilsen offer much by way of sights, the tastes are predictably marvelous, from a rainbow array of cold, pulpy *agua frescas* (fruit-flavored waters) to heaping mountains of spaghetti and flaming plates of *saganaki* (a sharp, hard cheese cut into wedges or squares and fried).

Akin to New York City's Meatpacking District, the West Loop is where Chicago finds its creative edge, with lower rents that allow restaurants, clubs and galleries to challenge the prime-time action of the Loop and Near North. Between meat-processing plants and art galleries, this neighborhood is just west of the Loop and a wholly more adventuresome place.

Outside of the West Loop, the Near West Side encompasses several ethnic enclaves that are worth a visit for the food. Chicago's Greektown occupies a few tight blocks of Hellenic restaurants, shops and bakeries along Halsted St, and Little Italy occupies a quaint stretch of Taylor St, where a stroll down the sidewalk will be scented with strong coffee and garlic.

A bit further south and even further southwest lies Pilsen, the center of Chicago's Mexican community, which is cluttered with murals and home to an excellent museum of Mexican art.

NEAR WEST SIDE & PILSEN

● SEE
Alto al Desplazamiento
  Urbano de Pilsen
  mural 1 C4
Chicago Blackhawks ..(see 30)
Chicago Bulls ....(see 30)
Cooper Academy
  murals 2 B4
Dejen Que Los Ninos Se
  Acerquen a Mi mural ..3 B5
Educacion – See y
  Know mural 4 B5
FLATFILE galleries 5 C1
Gulliver mural 6 B5
Haymarket Sq 7 D1
National Museum of
  Mexican Art 8 B4

Packer Schopf Gallery ...9 D1
Tony Wight Gallery 10 D1

⬛ SHOP
Athenian Candle Co 11 D2
Barbara's Bookstore 12 D3
Chicago Antique
  Market 13 C1
Pivot 14 C1
Self Conscious 15 C1

ⵙ EAT
Al's #1 Italian Beef 16 C3
Artopolis Bakery
  & Cafe 17 D2
Avec 18 D1

Blackbird 19 D1
Chez Joel 20 C3
Lou Mitchell's 21 D2
Mario's 22 C3
Mr Greek Gyros 23 D2
Nuevo Leon 24 B4
Parthenon 25 D2
Publican 26 D1
Rosebud 27 B3
Sweet Maple Café 28 C3
Tufano's Vernon
  Park Tap 29 C3

⭐ PLAY
United Center 30 B2
Working Bikes
  Cooperative 31 A3

NEIGHBORHOODS

NEAR WEST SIDE & PILSEN

◉ SEE

◉ GARFIELD PARK CONSERVATORY

☎ 312-746-5100; www.garfield-conservatory.org; 300 N Central Park Blvd; admission free; ⏱ 9am-5pm Fri-Wed, to 8pm Thu; Ⓜ Green Line to Conservatory

With 4.5 acres under glass, this is Chicago Park District's pride and joy; built in 1907, the conservatory's multi-million-dollar restoration campaign was completed in 2000, restoring it above and beyond its original splendor. One of the original designers, Jens Jensen, intended for the palms, ferns and other plants to re-create Chicago's prehistoric landscape. Newer halls contain displays of seasonal plants, which are especially spectacular in the weeks before Easter, and a hands-on children's garden lets kids play with plants that aren't rare or irreplaceable. A Demonstration Garden was added in 2002 to help answer the questions of the wide-eyed urban gardeners who come here. If you drive, lock up: the neighborhood isn't the safest. To get to the conservatory, follow W Lake St west to Garfield Park. Look for the glass structure north of the intersection of N Central Park.

◉ HAYMARKET SQUARE

Desplaines St btwn Lake & Randolph Sts; Ⓜ Green Line to Clinton

The best homage to the lunch break or eight-hour work day is a trip to Haymarket Sq, where an odd-looking bronze statue of guys on a wagon marks the spot where the labor movement began. On May 4, 1886, striking factory workers held a meeting here, which attracted police and quickly degenerated into chaos – a bomb exploded, police fired shots into the dispersing crowd, dozens were killed or injured and, eventually, four protesters were hung. August Spies uttered the famous words that would later appear on posters and flyers around the world: 'The day will come,' he said from beneath his hood, 'when our silence will be more powerful than the voices you are throttling today.'

◉ NATIONAL MUSEUM OF MEXICAN ART

☎ 312-738-1503; www.nationalmuseumofmexicanart.org; 1852 W 19th St; admission free; ⏱ 10am-5pm Tue-Sun; Ⓜ Blue Line to 18th St

Founded in 1982, this vibrant museum has become one of the best in the city. Housed in a renovated field house, the gleaming exhibit space tackles a bewilderingly complex task (summing up 1000 years of Mexican art and culture), and pulls it off beautifully. The museum also sponsors readings by top authors and performances by musicians and artists.

Nancy Villafranca
Pilsen native, DePaul graduate and Director of Education at the
National Museum of Mexican Art

First impression of the National Museum of Mexican Art (opposite)
Before you even come in, you're drawn to the Mayan motif, and this unique museum building located in the heart of the community. When you enter, there is a mural by one of our Chicago artists, Mario Castillo, that tells a visual history of his ancestors. **On Chicago's ethnic neighborhoods** Chicago has so many cultures living here, flourishing alongside each other, and there's a back and forth between mainstream and ethnic communities. Many people visit the museum for the flavor of a Mexican community. You could pick almost any other culture and learn something about it: go to Chinatown or some of the other ethnic neighborhoods. **On murals** They're a good way to know you're in a Latino community. It started with paintings on interior walls of temples and for hundreds of years this tradition has evolved.

⊙ WEST LOOP GALLERIES

near cnr Peoria & Washington Sts; M **Green Line to Clinton**

Tucked between meatpacking plants and warehouses, the galleries of the West Loop are the benchmark for contemporary art in Chicago. Most venues are located about three-quarters of a mile from the Green Line's Clinton stop, and are awkward to reach via public transportation; consider a cab. Gallery hours run from 11am to 5pm, Tuesday to Saturday; admission is free. For more information, check out the Snapshots chapter (above) and www.westloop.org. Some of our favorites out of the dozen or so galleries include **Tony Wight Gallery** (☎ 312-492-7261; ttp://tonywightgallery .com; 119 N Peoria St), **FLATFILE galleries** (☎ 312-491-1190; www.flatfilegalleries .com; 217 N Carpenter St) and **Packer Schopf Gallery** (☎ 312-226-8984; www .packergallery.com; 942 W Lake St).

🛍 SHOP

🏠 ATHENIAN CANDLE CO

Religious Items

☎ 312-332-6988; 300 S Halsted St; 🕑 closed Wed & Sun; M Blue Line to UIC-Halsted

Whether you're hoping to get lucky at bingo, remove a jinx or fall in love, this store promises to help with its array of candles, incense, love potions and miracle oils. It's been making candles for the city's Orthodox churches on-site since 1919, but isn't devoted to just one religion: you'll also find Buddha, the Pope and tarot cards.

🏠 BARBARA'S BOOKSTORE

Bookstore

☎ 312-413-2665; www.barbarasbook store.com; 1218 S Halsted St; 🚌 8

For serious fiction, no one can touch this locally owned store. Staff members have read what they sell, and touring authors regularly give readings.

🏠 CHICAGO ANTIQUE MARKET *Antiques*

☎ 312-951-9939; www.chicago antiquemarket.com; 1350 W Randolph St; admission $8; 🕑 9am-5pm last Sat & Sun of the month May-Oct; 🚌 20, or free trolley hourly from Tribune Tower, 435 N Michigan Ave

Packed with some 200 dealers, here you can pick up a trunkload of collectibles, costume jewelry, furniture, books, Turkish rugs and pinball machines. One of the coolest facets is the Indie Designer Fashion Market, where the city's fledgling designers sell their one-of-a-kind pieces. Hard-core junk hounds pay $20 to get first crack at the goods from 7:30am to 9am on Saturday.

📷 PIVOT *Clothing & Accessories*
☎ 312-243-4754; www.pivotboutique
.com; 1101 W Fulton Market; ⏱ closed
Mon; Ⓜ Green Line to Clinton

About as opposite as you can get
from neighboring Self Conscious,
Pivot is a sleek shop dealing in
ecofriendly fabrics, such as soft
bamboo T-shirts, and other green-
friendly gear. Even the shopping
bags (50% recycled content) and
clothing racks (made of reclaimed
wood and steel) were created ac-
cording to sustainable principles.

📷 SELF CONSCIOUS
Sportswear
☎ 312-633-4000; 1021 W Lake St;
Ⓜ Green Line to Clinton

Sneaker freaks, professional
athletes and hip-hop stars browse
through hoodies, track jackets
and T-shirts in this converted
West Loop warehouse. The ultra-
limited-edition Adidas and Nikes
are the main attraction, such as
the $2000 crocodile-and-
Italian-leather Nike Air Force
Ones, complete with an 18-karat
gold shoelace ornament.

🍴 EAT

🍴 AL'S #1 ITALIAN BEEF
Italian $
☎ 312-226-4017; www.alsbeef.com;
1079 W Taylor St; mains $3-5; Ⓜ Blue
Line to Racine

The original location of this legendary local chain is not the place to
grab lunch if you want to get off
your feet – there are no tables, only
a stand-up counter – but the legendary namesake sandwiches are
a favorite of Hillary Clinton (who
ordered them for her 50th birthday
party). Piled high with savory beef
that soaks through the thick bun,
the inexpensive treat is one of the
city's culinary hallmarks.

🍴 ARTOPOLIS BAKERY &
CAFE *Greek* $$
☎ 312-559-9000; 306 S Halsted St;
mains $6-14; Ⓜ Blue Line to UIC-Halsted

Like a good Greek salad, this place
has many ingredients: one of the
city's top bakeries – many of the
nearby Randolph St joints get
their bread here – selling oozing
baklava for $1.50; a café-bar that
opens onto the street, with tables
along the front; and a food bar
with classics such as spinach pie,
which you can eat in or get to go.

🍴 AVEC *New American* $$
☎ 312-377-2002; 615 W Randolph St;
mains $8-18; ⏱ closed lunch; Ⓜ Green
Line to Clinton

Feeling social? This casual cousin
to neighboring Blackbird gives
diners a chance to rub elbows at
eight-person communal tables.
Dishes are meant for sharing
(though you only have to share

with people you know), and the food from chef Koren Grieveson is exceptional. Sweet and savory, the bacon wrapped dates are the must on the menu.

🍴 BLACKBIRD
New American $$$
☎ 312-715-0708; www.blackbirdres taurant.com; 619 W Randolph St; mains $26-32; 🕐 closed lunch Sat, closed Sun; Ⓜ Green Line to Clinton

One of the most talked-about restaurants in town, this chic dining destination for Chicago's young and wealthy perches atop best-of lists for its exciting, notably seasonal menu. The warm-ups – such as the confit of suckling pig with concord grapes, chioggia beets and house-made prosciutto – are a perfect introduction to the visionary main dishes, which pair well with the short but careful wine list.

🍴 CHEZ JOEL *French* $$
☎ 312-226-6479; www.chezjoelbistro .com; 1119 W Taylor St; mains $15-24; Ⓜ Blue Line to Racine

Whether dining outside under the big oak tree, or in a cozy corner, atmosphere and exceptional French fare make Chez Joel – the renowned namesake of chef Joel Kazouini – a romantic favorite, though it's an odd duck on predominantly Italian Taylor St.

The menu is anchored by bistro favorites such as duck leg confit and coq au vin, and is complemented by an extensive wine list.

🍴 LOU MITCHELL'S *Breakfast* $
☎ 312-939-3111; www.loumitchellsres taurant.com; 565 W Jackson Blvd; mains $5-9; 🕐 lunch; Ⓜ Blue Line to Clinton

Immediately west of the Loop and close to Union Station, this coffee shop packs tourists elbow to elbow for greasy-spoon breakfasts. The omelets hang off the plates, and the fluffy flapjacks and crisp waffles are prepared with practiced perfection. Cups of coffee are bottomless, just like the charm of the staff who hand out free treats.

The talk of the town: slick and stylish Blackbird

🍴 MARIO'S *Italian Ice* $

1068 W Taylor St; ices $2-4; 🕐 **May-Oct;** Ⓜ **Blue Line to UIC-Halsted**

At this cheerful box-front store, super Italian ice comes loaded with big chunks of fresh fruit, and keeps crowds coming in the summer.

🍴 MR GREEK GYROS *Greek* $

☎ **312-906-8731; 234 S Halsted St; mains $4-7;** 🕐 **24hr;** Ⓜ **Blue Line to UIC-Halsted**

Although there's no sign of Mrs or Ms Greek, 'the Mr' is a classic gyro joint with good prices. While the fluorescent lighting and plastic decor may lack a little charm, the gyros have a beauty all their own. A full tasty meal comes in at just over $5, and it's open 24 hours a day.

🍴 NUEVO LEON *Mexican* $$

☎ **312-421-1517; 1515 W 18th St; mains $7-14;** Ⓜ **Blue Line to 18th St**

This huge place is a well-deserved tour stop, and tourists are well outnumbered by the Latino families who fill up the tables. Outstanding tacos, tamales and enchiladas are available, though the dish most likely to blow any meat-eater's taste buds is the *assado de puerco* – tender roast pork served with homemade flour tortillas. The breakfast is also excellent.

🍴 PARTHENON *Greek* $$

☎ **312-726-2407; 314 S Halsted St; mains $8-17;** Ⓜ **Blue Line to UIC-Halsted**

This veteran has anchored Greektown for three decades, hearing countless yells of '*Opa!*' to accompany the flaming *saganaki*. Greeks returning to the city from their suburban retreats have made this place a favorite. A plus for drivers: there's free valet service.

🍴 PUBLICAN *New American* $$$

☎ **312-733-9555; www.thepublican restaurant.com; 837 W Fulton Market; mains $15-25;** 🕐 **dinner;** Ⓜ **Blue Line to UIC-Halsted**

OK, so the decor is kind of weird (the long wood tables and spacey chandeliers bring to mind a futuristic Medieval Times), but the artful combination of fancy Belgian and Euro beer and pork-laden family-style dishes is conceptually flawless. The masterminds behind this place have two other excellent restaurants in the neighborhood: Avec and Blackbird. Given the whole-hog approach, vegetarians are going to struggle.

🍴 ROSEBUD *Italian* $$

☎ **312-942-1117; www.rosebudres taurants.com; 1500 W Taylor St; mains $14-22;** Ⓜ **Blue Line to Polk**

This location in Little Italy is the first branch of an empire of quality Italian restaurants that spread

THE WALLS OF PILSEN

Though Chicago is celebrated for ambitious public-art programs, Pilsen offers Chicago's most community-oriented open-air gallery experience, with varied and vibrant murals, often by local artists, depicting the social, religious and political issues that face its community. The best way to enjoy them is to join local muralist Jose Guerrero's **Pilsen Mural Tours** (☎ 773-342-4191); tours are approximately one hour, by appointment. 'It's important to realize that there is no art for art's sake,' Guerrero says of his neighborhood's murals. 'All art has political and social content.' Here are some of Guerrero's favorites.

> 18th St Station, CTA Pink/Blue Line – with the help of his students, Francisco Mendoza, a local art teacher, made this the most riotously colorful station on the CTA line, covering the walls in religious and cultural imagery.

> *Gulliver* (corner 19th and Cullerton Sts) – the outside of the home studio of artist Hector Duarte depicts the hero of Jonathan Swift's *Gulliver's Travels* tied down by barbed wire in a field of corn – a commentary on the challenges that face immigrants in America. The large scale makes viewers the size of Gulliver's captors.

throughout the city. It is popular with politicos and old-school Taylor St Italians who slurp down colossal piles of pasta and spinach gnocchi soaked in red sauces. Bring a big appetite.

🍴 SWEET MAPLE CAFÉ
Southern, Breakfast $

☎ 312-243-8908; 1339 W Taylor St; mains $7-11; ⏰ 7am-2pm Mon-Sun; Ⓜ Blue Line to Racine

The creaking floorboards, matronly staff and soulful home cookin' lend the Sweet Maple Café the bucolic appeal of a roadside Southern diner. The signature dishes – inch-thick banana (or, seasonally, peaches and cream) pancakes, cheddar grits and fluffy, fresh-baked biscuits that come smothered in spicy sausage gravy or as

part of a fried 'Chick'n Egg and Cheesier' – earn the superlatives of locals, but the egg dishes, sturdy muffins and lunch sandwiches are done with equal aplomb. If you only have time for one breakfast in the city, this is the place.

🍴 TUFANO'S VERNON PARK TAP *Italian* $$

☎ 312-733-3393; 1073 W Vernon Park Pl; mains $8-14; ⏰ closed lunch Sat & Sun, closed Mon; Ⓜ Blue Line to Polk

Still family-run after three generations, Tufano's serves old-fashioned, hearty Italian fare for modest prices. The blackboards carry a long list of daily specials, which can include such wonderful items as pasta with garlic-crusted broccoli. Amid the usual celebrity photos on the wall, you'll see some

> *Alto al Desplazamiento Urbano de Pilsen* (corner 18th and Bishop Sts) – the English translation of this expansive mural, a politically poignant collaboration between two key Pilsen muralists, Jose Guerrero and Hector Duarte, is 'Stop the Gentrification of Pilsen.' Community members are joined by portraits of Zapata and Cesar Chavez.
> *Dejen Que Los Ninos Se Acerquen a Mi* (corner Ashland Ave and Cullerton St) – slightly creepy photorealism and surreal juxtapositions define the murals by Jeff Zimmerman. This one depicts a priest holding a Latina baby girl aloft, speaking to the importance of faith in the community. Another of Zimmerman's murals worth seeking out is *Educacion – See y Know*, which you'll find a few blocks away at the corner of 21st St and Blue Island.
> Murals at the Cooper Academy (corner 19th and Bishop Sts) – the walls of the Cooper Elementary Dual Language Academy School host one of the neighborhood's most impressive works by Francisco Mendoza, a set of vivid mosaic portraits of Latino icons such as Jose Marti, Guadalupe Reyes and Lalo Guerrero.

really nice shots of Joey Di Buono and his family and their patrons through the decades.

⭐ PLAY
⭐ UNITED CENTER *Stadium*
☎ 312-455-4650; www.unitedcenter.com; 1901 W Madison St; 🚌 19
Built for $175 million and opened in 1992, this arena is home to the Bulls and the Blackhawks, and is the venue for special events such as the circus. The statue of an airborne Michael Jordan in front of the east entrance pays a lively tribute to the man whose talents financed the edifice. The center, surrounded by parking lots, is OK by day but gets pretty edgy at night – unless there's a game on, in which case squads of cops are everywhere to ensure public safety.

⭐ WORKING BIKES COOPERATIVE *Bike Shop*
☎ 312-421-5048; www.workingbikes.org; 1125 S Western Ave; 🕐 noon-5pm Wed, Sat & Sun; Ⓜ Blue Line to Western
If you'd like to cruise around for more than a day, consider buying a beater bike at this excellent nonprofit bike recycler. Prices range from $40 to $200 and proceeds go to sending bikes to needy individuals overseas. Plus, when you're ready to go home, you can recycle it right back to them.

>SOUTH LOOP & NEAR SOUTH SIDE

South Loop is where a campus of three worthy sights – the Field Museum, Shedd Aquarium and Adler Planetarium – sit side by side on the lakeshore, alongside the relatively tranquil 12th St Beach. Cafés and restaurants have finally colonized the area nearest these, so you no longer have to starve after your trip to one of the museums. If you look beyond the lovely museum campus, you'll see the luxury condos that have sprouted up everywhere in the South Loop, and with them the neighborhood is rapidly developing from its rough past. Blues fans will want to make the pilgrimage further into the neighborhood (probably by car), as there are some notable stages dotted through the area. Also, Northerly Island offers the city's closest thing to a genuine nature experience, with expansive, breezy views of the lake in the summer and tons of snowy family events through the winter. This part of town is also home to Chicago's small but busy Chinatown, where pork buns, steaming bowls of noodles and imported wares reward an afternoon of exploring.

SOUTH LOOP & NEAR SOUTH SIDE

Please see over for map

◎ SEE

◎ ADLER PLANETARIUM & ASTRONOMY MUSEUM

☎ 312-922-7827; www.adler planetarium.org; 1300 S Lake Shore Dr; adult/4-17yr $10/6, plus $13 for sky show, selected Mon & Tue Sep-Feb admission free; ⏲ 9:30am-6pm Jun-Aug, to 4:30pm Sep-May; 🚌 146

This, the first planetarium built in the western hemisphere, has been beautifully updated, with a digital sky show re-creating supernovas and mysteries of the solar system. Interactive exhibits allow you to simulate cosmic events such as a meteor hitting the earth. If you're interested in seeing another nearby museum, know that this place can easily be covered in less than two hours. If you're in no rush, chill out in the planetarium's garden.

◎ CHINATOWN

cnr Cermak Rd & Wentworth Ave; Ⓜ Red Line to Cermak-Chinatown

Once you get your bearings, Chinatown's charm is best enjoyed by going from bakery to bakery, nibbling almond cookies and sipping tea, and exploring the shops of imported goods. Essentially, there are two Chinatowns. The older, more authentic one stretches along Wentworth Ave south of Cermak; it's a commercial district more geared for residents than tourists. Chinatown Sq, along Archer Ave north of Cermak, is the newer, more touristy district. It fills an open-air mall with Chinese restaurants and shops, conveniently just steps off the Red Line.

◎ FIELD MUSEUM OF NATURAL HISTORY

☎ 312-922-9410; www.fieldmuseum .org; 1400 S Lake Shore Dr; adult/4-11yr $12/7, some exhibits extra, selected Mon & Tue Sep-Feb admission discounted; ⏲ 9am-5pm, last admission 4pm; 🚌 146

You may have it in mind to try rushing off to the far corners of this museum, but when you meet the *Tyrannosaurus rex* named Sue, a 13ft-tall, 41ft-long beast

The Field Museum's Greek temple-like entrance

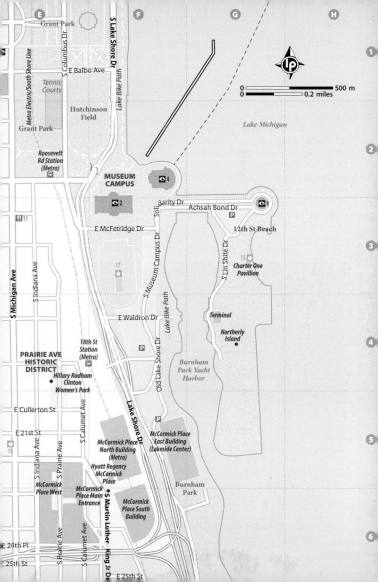

(the most complete *T rex* ever discovered), she'll stop you in your tracks. The old girl is a menacing guardian of the museum's entrance. 'Evolving Planet' has more of the big guys and gals. A clever display of Field artifacts helps the 'Inside Ancient Egypt' exhibit re-create an Egyptian burial chamber on three levels. 'Underground Adventure,' a vast exhibit exploring the habitats of animals and insects that live underground, also tops the attractions.

MUSEUM OF CONTEMPORARY PHOTOGRAPHY

☎ 312-663-5554; www.mocp.org; Columbia College, 600 S Michigan Ave; admission free; ☾ 10am-5pm Mon-Sat, to 8pm Thu, noon-5pm Sun; Ⓜ Red Line to Harrison

This museum focuses on American photography since 1937, and is the only institution of its kind between the coasts. The permanent collection includes the works of Debbie Fleming Caffery, Mark

Be mesmerized by the Caribbean Reef's watery show, Shedd Aquarium

Klett, Catherine Wagner, Patrick Nagatani and 500 more of the best photographers working today.

⊙ SHEDD AQUARIUM
☎ 312-939-2438; www.sheddaquarium.org; 1200 S Lake Shore Dr; pass to all exhibits adult/3-11yr $27.50/20.50, aquarium-only adult/3-11yr $8/6; ⏰ 9am-6pm Jun-Aug, to 10pm some Thu, reduced hours Sep-May; 🚌 146

There's something magical about standing in the dark corridors of the world's oldest aquarium, watching the animals float by. Though it could simply rest on its exceptional exhibits – say, beluga whales in a four-million-gallon aquarium – the Shedd makes a point of trying to tie concepts of ecosystems, food webs and marine biology into its presentation of amazing animals.

🏠 SHOP
🏠 NEW MAXWELL STREET MARKET *Market*
S Canal St btwn Taylor St & roughly 16th St; ⏰ 7am-3pm Sun; Ⓜ Blue Line to Clinton

If there's one shopping experience that stands at the opposite end of the orderly and expensive shops in the Magnificent Mile, this is it. Every Sunday morning hundreds of vendors set up stalls that sell everything from Cubs jerseys in

the wrong colors to 10-pack tube socks to tacos for $1. Take note that the market is not actually on Maxwell St, though it was for decades until the ever-sprawling University of Illinois at Chicago campus forced it to relocate.

🏠 TEN REN TEA & GINSENG
Food & Drink
☎ 312-842-1171; 2247 S Wentworth Ave; Ⓜ Red Line to Cermak-Chinatown

Ten Ren is the place to buy a spectrum of green, red, white and black teas, and the pots and accessories to serve them. You can also order bubble teas at the counter.

🏠 WOKS N THINGS *Homewares*
☎ 312-842-0701; 2234 S Wentworth Ave; Ⓜ Red Line to Cermak-Chinatown

This busy store carries every kind of Asian utensil and cookware you could want – pots, pans, wok brushes, knives.

🍴 EAT
🍴 JOY YEE'S NOODLE SHOP
Noodle House $
☎ 312-328-0001; 2159 S China Pl (Chinatown Sq); mains $6-12; Ⓜ Red Line to Cermak-Chinatown

You can order a colorful riot of bubble teas from the to-go counter at the door, but do yourself a favor by saving the deliciously sweet drinks for dessert after a bowl of udon (a thick, wheat-based noodle), *chow fun* (rice noodles) or chow mein.

🍴 LAO SZE CHUAN Chinese $$

☎ 312-326-5040; www.laoszechuan.com; 2172 S Archer Ave; mains $8-20; Ⓜ Red Line to Cermak-Chinatown

An authentic option in heavily touristy Chinatown Sq, the house special here is a three-chili chicken, though the extensive menu has excellent hot pots and recipes from the Szechuan province. If the choices are overwhelming, look for advice from watchful chef and owner 'Tony' Xiao Jun Hu.

Chow down at Joy Yee's Noodle Shop (p135)

🍴 LAWRENCE'S FISHERIES
Southern $

☎ 312-225-2113; www.lawrencesfisheries.com; 2120 S Canal St; mains $4-11; Ⓧ 24hr; Ⓜ Red Line to Cermak-Chinatown

This 24-hour fish-and-chips joint has a window framing a stunning scene of the Sears Tower over the Chicago River. But the order will still steal the show – popcorn shrimp, oysters, fish and chips, frog legs and other batter-crusted goodies. At night the parking lot outside of this typically family-oriented joint is a primo location for locals to sit on car hoods and shop for suspiciously current DVDs.

🍴 OPERA Asian Fusion $$

☎ 312-461-0161; 1301 S Wabash Ave; mains $14-25; Ⓧ closed lunch; Ⓜ Red Line to Roosevelt

With dramatic pan-Asian ambience, this upmarket Chinese restaurant serves up traditional plates – Peking duck, kung pao beef, general's chicken etc – remade with boutique meats, sharp spices and a light touch. Ask for the 'vault' seating constructed from old film-reel vaults.

🍴 PHOENIX Chinese $$

☎ 312-328-0848; 2131 S Archer Ave; mains $7-16; Ⓜ Red Line to Cermak-Chinatown

The draw here is the excellent dim sum: *char siu bao* (barbecued pork buns), shrimp-filled rice noodles and egg custards roll around the dining room in a seemingly endless parade of carts. The language barrier can be an issue, so keep in mind that if it looks like chicken feet, it probably is.

🍴 WAN SHI DA BAKERY
Chinese Bakery $
☎ 312-225-2113; 2229 S Wentworth St; mains $1-3; ⏰ 6am-10pm Mon-Fri; Ⓜ Red Line to Cermak-Chinatown
This bright bakery has fluffy pork buns, egg custards and coconut pastries, which make the best, and cheapest, à la carte lunch in Chinatown. Take it to go, or scarf it down at the pair of no-frills tables in back. The sister bakery across

the street, Chiu Quon Bakery, has a nearly identical menu.

🍸 DRINK
🍸 BERNICE'S TAVERN *Bar*
off Map pp132-3; ☎ 312-326-9460; 3238 S Halsted St; ⏰ 3pm-midnight Mon, 3pm-2am Wed-Fri, 11am-3am Sat, 11am-midnight Sun; 🚌 8
A motley assemblage of local artists and neighborhood regulars haunts this workaday Bridgeport tavern, where the eclectic calendar includes weekly metal DJs and a folkie open mic. Order enough Starka, a honey-flavored liqueur every bit as Lithuanian as the owners, and you'll likely get one on the house. To get here, head south on Halsted; it's just past the corner of 32nd St.

DIM SUM 101

If you're a little inexperienced, the language barrier, clattering train of steaming carts and general calamity can make going to dim sum brunch a bit daunting. To help you understand your *char siu bao* from your cow stomach, here are some definitions of key dishes in Chicago's Chinatown. Excellent dim sum dishes are available at **Phoenix** (opposite) and to-go from the bakeries along S Wentworth St.

> *Char siu bao* – these barbecue pork buns are a cornerstone dish of dim sum. They come in two varieties, with a dough casing that's either fluffy and steamed or golden and baked; they're both heavenly.

> *Shaomai* – these small, steamed dumplings are a savory pork mixture in a thin wheat-flour wrapper topped with crab roe and mushrooms.

> *Fung jao* – also known as 'phoenix talons,' this is the Chinese presentation of chicken feet. Suck off the skin and spit out the bones and cartilage.

> *Dan tat* – a sweet, flaky pastry filled with a sweet egg custard.

▼ SKYLARK *Bar*

☎ 312-948-5275; 2159 S Halsted St; 🚍 8

The Skylark is the place to end a long night after exploring southern reaches of the city. It's a bastion for artsy drunkards, who slouch into big booths sipping on strong drinks and eyeing the long room. It's at the corner of Halsted and Cermak.

⭐ PLAY

⭐ 12TH STREET BEACH *Beach*

1200 S Lake Shore Dr; 🚍 146

At the 12th St Beach, near the Adler Planetarium, you can climb the rocks to the breakwater for views of the lake. Despite the beach's proximity to the busy Museum Campus, the crescent-shaped sand sliver is bizarrely secluded. Beach bonus: if you can't get tickets to see your favorite band at Charter One Pavilion on Northerly Island, you can sit here and still hear the tunes.

⭐ BUDDY GUY'S LEGENDS
Blues Club

☎ 312-427-1190; www.buddyguys.com; 754 S Wabash Ave; cover usually $10-15; 🕙 11am-2am Mon-Fri, 5pm-3am Sat, 6pm-2am Sun; Ⓜ Red Line to Harrison

Located in a somewhat drab storefront, the talent that plays this stage is nothin' to discount, though deep fans of Chicago blues will probably be looking over their shoulder for the legendary guitar player whose name is on the door. Rest assured, Buddy himself does take the stage occasionally, but even if not, the quality of the music (and soul food) won't disappoint.

⭐ SOLDIER FIELD *Stadium*

☎ 312-235-7000; www.soldierfield.net; 1410 S Museum Campus Dr; 🚍 146

Home of the Bears, this oft-renovated edifice has been host to everything from civil rights speeches by Martin Luther King Jr to Brazilian soccer games. A 2003 makeover quickly saw it dubbed 'the Mistake on the Lake.' The landmark folks agreed and whacked it from their list, saying it

Waiting for the late set at Buddy Guy's

QUICK GUIDE TO CHICAGO BLUES JOINTS

With so many clubs to choose from, it can be tough to know where to find your particular shade of blues. Among our favorites:

> **Buddy Guy's Legends** (opposite) – the location and facade are a bit rough around the edges, but this is the best place to catch the legend himself.
> **Rosa's Lounge** (p119) – far away from the tourist masses, this scruffy club has loads of hard-core authenticity.
> **Blue Chicago** (p56) – the most polished of the city's blues clubs is near the heart of the Loop action.
> **Kingston Mines** (p76) – a constant wail comes off the two stages, perfect for indecisive ears.
> **New Checkerboard Lounge** (p145) – though it's housed in a strip mall, this club is spacious and good for grinding.
> **B.L.U.E.S.** (p76) – open 365 days a year, this intimate club lets you get close to the action.

jeopardized the national landmark integrity.

⭐ WILLIE DIXON'S BLUES HEAVEN *Museum, Blues Venue*
☎ 312-808-1286; www.bluesheaven
.com; 2120 S Michigan Ave; tours $10;
🕑 noon-3pm Mon-Fri, to 2pm Sat; 🚌 1
This humble building was home to legendary Chess Records, a temple of blues and a spawning ground of rock 'n' roll. Today Willie Dixon's Blues Heaven, a nonprofit group set up by the late bluesman, promotes a blues legacy in the space. A gift store is open in front, while the studios where Muddy Waters and Dixon recorded are upstairs. Visitors will meet AJ Tribble, Blues Heaven docent and Willie Dixon's nephew. Reservations required.

>HYDE PARK & SOUTH SIDE

Before it became known as Barack Obama's neighborhood, Hyde Park's reputation was all about the Gothic buildings and Nobel laureates of the University of Chicago campus, whose student population fills its cafés and defines its options for nightlife. It's a hike from downtown, situated within Chicago's hardscrabble South Side, but it has worthy sights if you're willing to make the trip, including a stunning example of Frank Lloyd Wright's 'Prairie School' style of architecture. The intersection of 57th St and S University Ave is a great place to start exploring the gargoyle-cluttered campus, where, among other things, the atomic age began. Hyde Park is also home to one of the city's most family-friendly museums, the Museum of Science and Industry, where curious exhibits include a live chick hatchery, industrial food production and an entire German U-boat that was captured during WWII.

Beyond Hyde Park, the South Side has its charms, though they take a little digging. Explorers will find neighborhoods that are slowly piecing things together in the shadow of some of the country's bleakest housing projects, the neglected flip side of the immaculately groomed city pictured in the pages of Mayor Daley's tourist brochures.

HYDE PARK & SOUTH SIDE

◎ SEE
Bond Chapel 1 B4
DuSable Museum of African
American History 2 A3
Museum of Science &
Industry 3 E4
Nuclear Energy
Sculpture 4 B3
Promontory Point 5 F3
Robie House 6 C4

Rockefeller Memorial
Chapel 7 C4
William Rainey Harper
Memorial Library 8 B4

🛍 SHOP
57th Street Books 9 C4
Seminary Cooperative
Bookstore 10 C4

🍴 EAT
Caffé Florian 11 D3
Dixie Kitchen & Bait
Shop 12 D2
Medici 13 C4

⭐ PLAY
Court Theatre 14 B3
New Checkerboard
Lounge 15 D2

500 m

0.2 miles

Lake Michigan

Lake Bike Path

Lake Shore Dr

Chicago Beach Dr

Jackson Park Beach

East Lagoon

West Lagoon

Columbia Dr

57th St Beach

Lake Shore Dr

S South Shore Dr

S Everett Ave

S East End Ave

S Cornell Ave

E Hyde Park Blvd

Lake Park Ave

S Blackstone Ave

Dorchester Ave

S Kimbark Ave

E 50th St

KENWOOD

E Hyde Park Blvd

Greenwood Ave

S Ellis Ave

Drexel Blvd

S Cottage Gve Ave

E 50th St

Langley Ave

Champlain Ave

53rd St Station (Metro)

E Park Blvd

S Cornell Ave

S 53rd St

S 54th St

S 55th St

S 56th St

55th-56th-57th St Station (Metro)

S Harper Ave

S Blackstone Ave

S Dorchester Ave

S Ridgewood Ct

S Kenwood Ave

S Woodlawn Ave

S University Ave

S Greenwood Ave

S Ellis Ave

S Ingleside Ave

S Drexel Ave

S Cottage Gve Ave

Payne Dr

E Drexel Square

E 52nd St

E 53rd St

S 52nd St

S 53rd St

S 54th St

S 55th St

S 55th Pl

S 56th Pl

E 57th St

E 58th St

SOUTH SIDE & HYDE PARK

HYDE PARK

S Harper Ave

S Blackstone Ave

S Dorchester Ave

E 58th St

Ida Noyes Hall

E 59th St

59th St Station (Metro)

S Stony Island Ave

Chicago Theological Seminary

President's House

N Midway Plaisance

Joseph Regenstein Library

University of Chicago Administration Building Tower

Chicago Anatomy Building Group

Cummings Life Sciences Center

Culver Hall/Cobb Hall/Court

Eckhart Hall

University of Chicago

Swift Hall

Pick Hall

Goodspeed Hall

University of Chicago Hospital

Payne Dr

👁 SEE

📷 DUSABLE MUSEUM OF AFRICAN AMERICAN HISTORY

☎ 773-947-0600; www.dusable museum.org; 740 E 56th Pl; adult/6-13yr $3/1, Sun admission free; 🕙 10am-5pm Tue-Sat, noon-5pm Sun; 🚌 4

In a peaceful part of Washington Park, this newly expanded museum features permanent exhibits that cover African American experiences from slavery through the Civil Rights movement. The museum, housed in a 1910 building, takes its name from Chicago's first permanent settler,

Jean Baptiste Pointe Du Sable, a French-Canadian of Haitian descent (see p172).

📷 MUSEUM OF SCIENCE & INDUSTRY

☎ 773-684-1414; www.msichicago.org; cnr 57th St & S Lake Shore Dr; adult/3-11yr $11/7; 🕙 9:30am-4pm Mon-Sat, 11am-4pm Sun, to 5:30pm Jun-Aug; 🚌 6, Ⓜ Metra to 55th-56th-57th St Station

Sure, the nine permanent exhibits of this enormous museum examine just about every aspect of life on Earth, but its pleasures are in the details: chicks struggling to

UNIVERSITY OF CHICAGO & THE NOBEL PRIZE

Best pack your thinking cap for your tour of the University of Chicago; the place is a veritable factory of Nobel laureates, many in the field of economics and physics. Here are but a few of the institution's faculty, researchers and alumni who have won a Nobel Prize.

> Albert A Michelson – the first American Nobel laureate in the sciences, Michelson was honored with a 1907 Prize for Physics for measuring the speed of light.
> Willard Libby – Libby's radiocarbon dating system revolutionized archaeological dating and won him a Nobel Prize for Chemistry in 1960.
> Charles Huggins – in 1966 Huggins got a Nobel Prize for discovering that hormones could control some forms of cancer.
> Milton Friedman – he won a 1976 Nobel Prize in Economic Sciences for his theory that stressed the role of the private sector, not government, in economic stability.
> Saul Bellow – Bellow won a Nobel Prize for Literature in 1976; his Chicago-themed works stressed the disorienting nature of contemporary society.
> Subrahmanyan Chandrasekhar – the nephew of Indian Nobel laureate Sir C V Raman (some brains in that family!), Chandrasekhar won a Nobel Prize for Physics in 1983 for his role in understanding the evolution and structure of stars.
> Yoichiro Nambu – this Japanese-born researcher and professor won a Nobel Prize for Physics in 2008 for his study of theoretical physics that helps explain the behavior of nature's fundamental particles.

peck their way out of shells in the baby chick hatchery, the whimsical little high jinks of wooden puppets in the Cabaret Mechanical Theatre and the minuscule furnishings in Colleen Moore's fairy castle. If you want to go big, explore the German U-boat captured during WWII ($5 extra to tour it), take a (rather frightening) tour through industrial agriculture, or climb into the life-size shaft of a coal mine.

⊙ ROBIE HOUSE

☎ 773-834-1847; www.wrightplus.org; 5757 S Woodlawn Ave; ⏰ 11am-3pm Sat; Ⓜ Metra to 55th-56th-57th St Station

It might be a hike, but Frank Lloyd Wright's brilliant Robie House is the most famous and stunning example of 'Prairie School' design and often listed among the most important structures in American architecture. The low horizontal planes and dramatic cantilevers were meant to mirror the Midwestern landscape. At the time of publishing, the house was undergoing extensive restoration, which had disrupted the tour schedule, so call ahead.

⊙ UNIVERSITY OF CHICAGO

☎ 773-702-1234; www.uchicago.edu; 5801 S Ellis Ave; 🚌 6, Ⓜ Metra to 55th-56th-57th St Station

Imposing architecture at University of Chicago

John D Rockefeller was a major contributor to this premiere American university, donating more than $35 million to the school that opened its doors in 1892. The Gothic campus will bring to mind the schools of Europe, with particularly beautiful sights in the **Rockefeller Memorial Chapel** (5850 S Woodlawn Ave), the **William Rainey Harper Memorial Library** (1116 E 59th St) and the **Bond Chapel** (1050 E 59th St). On Ellis Ave, between 56th and 57th, sits the 1968 Henry Moore bronze sculpture *Nuclear Energy*. This marks the spot where Enrico Fermi and company started the nuclear age by harnessing the power of splitting an atom.

SHOP

57TH STREET BOOKS
Bookstore
☎ 773-684-1300; http://semcoop.book
sense.com; 1301 E 57th St; Ⓜ Metra to
55th-56th-57th St Station
A serious university demands a
serious bookstore, and as you descend the stairs to this basement-
level shop, you'll know you're in
the right place. Its labyrinth of
low-slung rooms makes up the
kind of old-fashioned bookstore
that goes way deeper than the
popular titles. It has excellent
staff picks and an exhaustive
travel section. Seminary Co-op is
the sister shop selling academic
tomes.

SEMINARY COOPERATIVE
BOOKSTORE *Bookstore*
☎ 773-752-4381; http://semcoop
.booksense.com; 5757 S University Ave;
Ⓜ Metra to 55th-56th-57th St Station
This is the bookstore of choice for
several University of Chicago Nobel Prize winners, including Robert
Fogel, who says, 'For a scholar, it's
one of the great bookstores of the
world.' The shop is owned by the
same folks as 57th Street Books.

EAT

CAFFÉ FLORIAN *American* $
☎ 773-752-4100; 1450 E 57th St; mains
$6-11; Ⓜ Metra to 59th St Station
The best food on the edges of
campus is served in this busy café,

OBAMA'S CHICAGO

> **Chase Tower** (Map pp38–9, D3) – at a law firm in this 60-story building is where he
  met his future wife, Michelle Robinson.
> **Law School, University of Chicago** (p143) – this is where President Obama taught law
  for a decade, starting in 1993.
> **57th Street Books** (above) – with its big selection of children's books, this bookstore
  was named by Michelle Obama as the family's favorite for browsing.
> **Topolobampo** (p54) – Rick Bayless' masterful, seasonal Mexican plates were a favorite
  of the couple; they would start things off with tortilla soup and guacamole, and enjoy
  margaritas made tableside.
> **Dixie Kitchen & Bait Shop** (opposite) – while in the state senate, Obama sang the
  praises of this place on 'Check, Please!', a public TV show featuring amateur restaurant
  reviews. The show never ran (producers thought Obama was too polished for the
  amateurs-only show) but his full, glowing review is up on YouTube.
> **Promontory Point** – Obama used to shoot hoops at the outdoor courts here with his
  brother-in-law, Craig Robinson, a basketball coach at the University of Oregon.

where black-bean nachos, fish and chips and Italian items are highlights of the menu.

🍴 DIXIE KITCHEN & BAIT SHOP *Southern* $$
☎ 773-363-4943; www.dixiekitchen chicago.com; 5225 S Harper Ave; mains $7-16; ⏰ 11am-10pm Sun-Thu, to 11pm Fri & Sat; 🚌 6

After the Gothic hallows of the University of Chicago, the oddball Southern memorabilia at this Dixie eatery is a homey delight – even if it feels a bit misplaced at the edge of an aging strip mall. Despite the name, there's no fish food here. Start with complimentary biscuits and mini cornbread loaves, then order fried green tomatoes, crawfish and cornbread fritters, or a cup of gumbo. For more quality Southern fare, try an oyster po'boy or the reliable country fried steak.

🍴 MEDICI *American* $$
☎ 773-667-7394; 1327 E 57th St; mains $6-14; Ⓜ Metra to 59th St Station

The menu of thin-crust pizzas, sandwiches and salads draws UC students to this colorful café and bakery. For breakfast, try the 'eggs espresso,' made by steaming eggs in an espresso machine. After

your meal, check the vast bulletin board out front. It's the perfect place to size up the character of the community.

⭐ PLAY

⭐ COURT THEATRE *Theater*
☎ 773-753-4472; www.courttheatre .org; 5535 S Ellis Ave; Ⓜ Metra to 55th-56th-57th St Station

A classical company hosted by the University of Chicago, the Court focuses on great works from the Greeks to Shakespeare, and various international plays not often performed in the US.

⭐ NEW CHECKERBOARD LOUNGE *Blues Club*
☎ 773-684-1472; 5201 S Harper Ct; 🚌 15

When the original location of this Bronzeville blues room closed in 2003, enthusiasts mourned – until it reopened in this bigger, better-sounding space in Hyde Park. The new location is more inviting for university kids who often join locals for quality local and national electric blues acts. The cover varies with the reputation of the performers on stage and so does the start time, so call ahead.

>SNAPSHOTS

It takes a thick skin to survive the long Chicago winter and an open mind to understand its character. But for more than just weather, this ain't no place for the faint hearted, so ditch the tourist staples and explore: Chicago's biggest rewards wait just under the surface.

Golden, postcard city views from North Avenue Beach (p77), Old Town

SNAPSHOTS

ACCOMMODATIONS

From dramatic views and rose-petal bubble baths to hostel bunks and homestays, you'll have no problem finding amenities at every level in Chicago. There are some 35,000 hotel rooms in the city. Finding something at a reasonable rate? Good luck. Being the biggest city in the Midwest and convention central, demand is high year-round, and it gets downright impossible to find value on summer weekends when the festival season and tourism peak. If you're willing to be flexible with your dates, you'll have a better chance of finding a place to stay that won't break the bank.

Since Chicago covers over 225 sq miles, let your interests narrow things down a bit. If you're going to tromp up and down the Mag Mile and binge on shopping, the Gold Coast or slightly more moderately priced Near North are the places to lay your head. If you're interested in taking in the magnificent buildings and museums of the Loop and South Loop, there are plenty of options in the heart of the city, many of which are very close to El train stops that can whisk you away to quieter outlying neighborhoods. These areas of town have the greatest concentration of hotels.

To really explore Chicago's neighborhoods, consider a quieter stay at a bed and breakfast – especially ones in historic homes in Wicker Park, Andersonville, Wrigleyville and Lake View – which usually offer free internet and free parking. Investigating a vacation rental is particularly ideal for traveling families; the price of an apartment with more space and homey amenities is often cheaper and more comfortable than a hotel room.

Generally speaking, if you're only concerned with the price, there are a few good options in the South Loop and further south, some overlooking

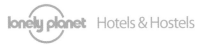

Need a place to stay? Find and book it at lonelyplanet.com. Over 132 properties are featured for Chicago – each personally visited, thoroughly reviewed and happily recommended by a Lonely Planet author. From hostels to high-end hotels, we've hunted out the places that will bring you unique and special experiences. Read independent reviews by authors and other travelers, and get practical information including amenities, maps and photos. Then reserve your room simply and securely via Hotels & Hostels – our online booking service. It's all at lonelyplanet.com/hotels.

the lakefront or near the museum campuses. Using search engines, you're likely to find the most affordable chain options close to Chicago's airports. Even though these are connected by reliable public transportation, it's worth it to put down a little extra to spare a long commute. Also, be mindful about parking prices when choosing a downtown hotel, as they won't show up in your quote. It's possible to get a great rate using one of the deal finders' favorite sites (lookin' at you, Priceline), only to have the fee for parking your car double the price of your stay. Chicago's public transportation might not be the best in the US, but it's close and, especially in summer months, many neighborhoods' attractions are walkable.

PET FRIENDLY
> Palmer House Hilton (www.chicago hilton.com)
> Hotel Burnham (www.burnhamhotel .com)
> W Hotel Chicago-Lakeshore (www .whotels.com)
> Peninsula (www.peninsula.com)
> Hotel Monaco (www.monaco-chicago .com)

LAKE VIEWS
> W Hotel (www.whotels.com)
> Park Hyatt (http://parkchicago.hyatt .com)
> Drake Hotel (www.thedrakehotel.com)
> Congress Plaza Hotel (www.congress plazahotel.com)
> Swissôtel (www.swissotel.com)

GAY STAYS
> Villa Toscana (www.thevillatoscana .com)
> Ardmore House (www.ardmore housebb.com)
> Flemish House (www.chicagobandb .com)
> W Chicago City Center (www .starwoodhotels.com)

OVER-THE-TOP AMENITIES
> A $60,000 proposal package, with ring, at the James (www.jameshotels.com)
> A pet goldfish to borrow at the Hotel Monaco (www.monaco-chicago.com)
> The sound pillow with harmonic sleep CD at Affinia Chicago (www.affinia.com)
> A butler to walk your dog at the Peninsula (www.peninsula.com)
> A state-of-the-art home entertainment system at the Conrad Chicago (www.conradhotels.com)

TOP PICKS
> The James (www.jameshotels.com)
> Hotel Monaco (www.monaco-chicago .com)
> Hotel Burnham (www.burnhamhotel .com)
> Affinia Chicago (www.affinia.com)
> Peninsula (www.peninsula.com)

WEB RESOURCES
> www.chicagohotels.com
> www.chicago-bed-breakfast.com

ARCHITECTURE

The ubiquitous tale of the Chicago fire – which raged for three whole days in 1871, leveling 3 sq miles of bustling city – is kind of like the mild, Midwestern version of the story of the phoenix, the great fire bird that burned fiercely in order to be reborn. Both mythical and allegorical, the Chicago story involves Mrs Catherine O'Leary's cow (whose name is Madeline, Naomi, Daisy or Gwendolyn, depending on who's telling it), who was blamed for kicking over a lantern and starting the blaze.

Regardless of how it happened, the devastation of the Great Chicago Fire quickly turned into one of the young city's great blessings, as the moment in history and the location at the heart of a growing industrial nation ensured that Chicago would not merely be rebuilt. The flock of aspiring architects who raced each other toward the heavens rebuilt with the finest and most innovative structures the world had ever known.

From the oddball postmodernism of the mostly conceptual Chicago Spire to the artfully low-slung eves of Frank Lloyd Wright's Prairie Homes, Chicago's buildings don't allow you to pass by without telling their own stories. Many of them are told in the bold designs of young architects such as Dankmar Adler, Daniel Burnham, John Root and Louis Sullivan. These men saw the scorched Loop as a sandbox for innovation, and they rapidly built bigger, better commercial structures over the low buildings that immediately went up after the fire. These men and their colleagues made up the 'Chicago School' (who some say practiced the 'Commercial Style'), which stressed economy, simplicity and function. Using steel framing and high-speed elevators, they created their pinnacle achievement: the modern skyscraper. And the houses they built for themselves during this period are just about as interesting; the Prairie Ave Historic District (Map pp132–3, E4), with its majestic homes, was the most fashionable residential area in the city in the years after the fire.

Then it was off to the races. William Le Baron Jenney, the architect who constructed the world's first iron-and-steel-framed building in the 1880s, set up shop in Chicago, training a crop of architects that pushed the city skyward through internal frames. The Monadnock (Map pp38–9, D4) is a good place to get a practical sense of how quickly these innovations were catching on: the original northern half of the building consists of traditional load-bearing walls that are 6ft thick at the bottom, while the southern half, constructed only two years later, uses the then-revolutionary metal frame for drastically thinner walls that go just as high.

It was Louis Sullivan's apprentice, Frank Lloyd Wright, who endowed Chicago with its most distinctive style, the 'Prairie School', from a small studio in Oak Park. Wright's Prairie Homes contrasted the grand edifices of the Chicago School with their modest low-slung horizon lines, flat roofs, overhanging eaves, unadorned open spaces and natural materials that mirrored the Midwestern landscape. Excellent tours of Wright's structures, which dot the city and outlying suburbs, can be set up through the **Frank Lloyd Preservation Trust** (www.wrightplus.org). And though the city's monumental examples of the beaux arts and art deco movements are well documented in civic buildings dressed up in a mixed bag of Classical Roman and Greek elements, the city actually received its greatest modern architectural contribution in the years after WWII, when Ludwig Mies van der Rohe pioneered the new 'International Style.' The steel frame that once revolutionized the Chicago skyline was again seminal, though now no longer hidden on the inside of walls – the International Style was all about exposed metal and glass, and represents most people's image of the modern skyscraper. The best way to learn about Chicago's impressive parade of buildings is through a tour with the Chicago Architecture Foundation (p42), which operates a number of walking and bus tours in the Loop and other neighborhoods.

FIVE TO KNOW IN CHICAGO ARCHITECTURE

> Louis Sullivan – Chicago's architectural founding father
> Frank Lloyd Wright – Sullivan's student and one of America's leading architectural minds
> Ludwig Mies van der Rohe – stressed stylish and simple buildings that influenced Chicago's modern skyscrapers
> Frank Gehry – his work defines Millennium Park (p41)
> Santiago Calatrava – architect behind the Chicago Spire (p52)

READING UP ON THE SKYLINE

> *Chicago Architecture and Design,* Jay Pridmore and George Larson
> *Frank Lloyd Wright Field Guide,* edited by Marie Clayton
> *Masterpieces of Chicago Architecture,* John Zukowsky and Martha Thorne
> *Chicago's Famous Buildings,* Franz Schulze and Kevin Harrington

FOOD

With advance apologies to Chicago's growing foodie elite, the quintessential food experience in the city still takes the form of encased meat. No, it's not snapping through the skin of a Vienna Beef hot dog laden with peppers and pickles, however requisite an experience that is to visiting Chicago. It's the sophisticated, uptown offspring of the Chicago hot dog, a foie gras and sauternes duck sausage with truffle sauce *moutarde*, foie gras mousse and *sel gris* served at Hot Doug's (p117). No other menu item represents the past and present of Chicago's whimsical, traditional, adventurous culinary identity so well: a tasty, deliriously rich clash of high and low culture, at once traditional and visionary. From the pork-dominated decadence of Publican (p127) to the buttery tenderness of an aged porterhouse from Gibson's (p64), eating in this city is a largely carnivorous activity.

It can be an exhausting one as well. Just stare down a heavy-metal-themed, half-pound Angus burger smothered in cheddar, pulled pork and pickles (the 'Led Zepplin') at Kuma's Corner (p117) or a cheese-and-sausage-filled slice from Giordano's (p55) that's as thick as a Gutenberg bible, and you'll realize that you're unlikely to leave this vacation slimmer.

That's certainly not to say that the hulking plates of meat haven't spawned a notable backlash. The city's vegetarian juggernauts, such as Victory's Banner (p86) and the Chicago Diner (p84), have earned a cultish devotion through their creative meatless fare. A dynamic vanguard of Chicago chefs has also taken the lead on lighter fare, helming the growing 'molecular gastronomy' trend – a catch-all term for the exciting approach to meal preparation that's more like a science experiment (what exactly does a 'pillow of lavender air' taste like?). The refined tasting menu of Alinea (p73) and visionary plates at Charlie Trotter's (p73) are short-listed among the most innovative dinner menus in the world.

If getting an authentic taste of the city ranks high on your agenda, best to get out of the Loop. Restaurant-rich neighborhoods in the Near North, Gold Coast and Wicker Park have a concentration of great restaurants at their center. If you're willing to take a bit of a hike, the immigrant enclaves a bit further out still dish out the most affordable, authentic fare in Chicago, even beyond the heavily traveled precincts of Greektown and Little Italy. For starters, try the *jibarito*, a pork sandwich covered in garlicky mayo, served between thick, crispy slices of plantains at the Borinquen Restaurant (p115), or a bowl of steaming noodles at Joy Yee's Noodle Shop (p135).

If you speak to Chicago natives, you'll probably get a feel for the great debates that shape the civic dialogue around dinnertime: brunch and pizza. The former is Chicago's favorite meal of the week, and lines outside particularly brilliant brunch joints, such as M Henry (p96) and Sweet Maple Café (p128), twist out the door around noon on weekends. As for pizza, Chicago's ambassadorial deep-dish might be its most famous edible export, but which *particular* deep-dish is likely to stir a heated conversation.

But one thing's a fact: in the city of big shoulders, a restaurant has to earn its stripes – Chicago's diners aren't likely to jump on trendy food bandwagons that swoop in from either of the coasts, or blow smoke when you ask for opinions about where to grab lunch.

BEST THINGS TO EAT IN CHICAGO
> Slice of sausage pie from Pequod's Pizza (p74)
> Loaded hot dog from Clark Street Dog (p84)
> Porterhouse from Gibson's (p64)
> Tasting menu at Charlie Trotters (p73)
> Brunch at M Henry (p96)

HAUTE FOOD, CHICAGO STYLE
> Charlie Trotter's (p73)
> Alinea (p73)
> Blackbird (p126)
> Topolobampo (p54)
> West Town Tavern (p107)

CHEAP & PACKED WITH CHARACTER
> El Taco Veloz (p105)
> Billy Goat Tavern (p53)
> Weiner's Circle (p74)
> Al's #1 Italian Beef (p125)
> Wan Shi Da Bakery (p137)

VEGGIE DELIGHTS
> Chicago Diner (p84)
> Victory's Banner (p86)
> Green Zebra (p106)
> Lula Café (p118)

Top left The place to taste celebrity chef Rick Bayless' Mexican fare: Frontera Grill (p54)

SHOPPING

Your poor, poor feet. Just when they thought you were done after spending the day tromping up and down the Magnificent Mile with an increasingly heavy bundle of packages, you accidentally open to this page to discover that you've only seen the iceberg's tip with respect to the wealth of shopping opportunities in Chicago. The Mag Mile sings the shoppers' siren song as jingling cash registers accompany the age-old lyric: 'cash or charge?' The stretch of pavement on Michigan Ave in the Near North is stuffed silly with towering malls and high-end chains, such as Gucci, Louis Vuitton and Burberry. Things get festive around the winter holidays, with twinkling lights and plenty of window displays. But even though it may indeed be the most distinguished shopping area in town, it's only the beginning.

Just north, in the Gold Coast, things get a bit ritzier as top designers set up shop in the pricy boutiques on Oak St. North of that, more unique shopping opportunities come in Chicago's boutique-rich neighborhoods, such as Bucktown, where fashionistas float through the doors of the mid- to high-end boutiques of Milwaukee Ave (Map pp102–3, B4). In Wicker Park's Division St (Map pp102–3, C5), young, local designers offer one-of-a-kind wares, and Andersonville offers its own one-of-a-kind shops for kids and plenty of cute cafés to satisfy shoppers' hunger.

Even though this was the city that exported Crate & Barrel, Sears and Woolworths, its greatest strength for shoppers lies in its thriving culture of independent and family-run stores and a friendly Midwestern atmosphere. Record stores, new and retro fashions, art and architecture-related items and ethnic cargo are the city's most memorable merchandise. The city doesn't have a shopping experience more down-to-earth than the sprawling open-air bazaar at the New Maxwell Street Market (p135), where the vendors show up selling everything from power tools to European antiques, and a blues band keeps things lively.

If shopping is your main reason for coming to town, be sure to investigate the shopping blog at *Chicago Magazine* (www.chicagomag.com; click the 'Shopping' tab) or subscribe to its 'Sales Check' e-newsletter. Both list hot upcoming sales, new store openings and events.

ONLY-IN-CHICAGO SOUVENIRS
> City of Chicago Store (p62)
> Spice House (p72)
> Chicago Tribune Store (p53)
> Chicago Architecture Foundation Store (p42)
> New Maxwell Street Market (p135)

BOUTIQUES & ONE-OF-A-KIND STORES
> Strange Cargo (p83)
> Wolfbait & B-girls (p115)
> Pivot (p125)
> Habit (p106)
> Jazz Record Mart (p53)

Top left The curiously named Wolfbait & B-girls (p115) **Above** A Chicago indie-rock scene player: Reckless Records (p105)

SNAPSHOTS

VIEWS & VISTAS

Is it a giant ugly bug, or a baboon? Picasso never would say what the 1967 iron sculpture represents, but the Chicago landmark, **Untitled** (Map pp38-9; 50 W Washington St), is the perfect place to start a walking tour of downtown and come back home with a scrapbook full of postcard-quality snaps.

Cross the street to Miró's **Chicago** (Map pp38-9; 69 W Washington St), a robot/pagan-fertility-goddess-like sculpture that the Spanish artist unveiled in 1981. A few steps away, you can pose in front of the picture-perfect post-card shot – the six-story-high illuminated sign spelling the town's name. The 1920s marquee for the Chicago Theatre (p40) is one of downtown's classic shots.

Walk a few blocks north on State to find the clock at the old Marshall Field's (Map pp38-9, D2). 'Meeting under the clock' has been a Chicago tradition since 1897, when Marshall Field installed the elaborate ironwork timepiece at Washington and State. A group photo beneath the clock (the building now houses Macy's) is a must.

Pose under the 38ft-diameter Tiffany dome at the Chicago Cultural Center (p37), reputed to be the world's largest, before shooting across the street to snap some pics of *Cloud Gate,* aka 'The Bean' (see p41). Stand on the west side of the giant mirrored blob and hold your camera at waist level so you can take a self portrait with a skyline background.

From there, head to the front stairs of the Art Institute (p37), where two 1894 bronze lions stand – city mascots of sorts. They wore helmets when the Bears won the 1985 Superbowl and a White Sox cap during the 2005 pennant. Zoom in for a striking profile shot silhouetted against city buildings.

Alexander Calder's **Flamingo** (Map pp38-9, D4; plaza at Dearborn & Adams Sts) is another monumental piece of public art easily recognized in Chicago. That bright red paint job should photograph well, especially if you frame it against Mies van der Rohe's ground-breaking 1974 glass-and-steel Kluczynski Building in the Chicago Federal Center (Map pp38–9, D4).

Finally, get a shot of the 1450ft-tall Sears Tower (p41), the tallest US building (pre– and post–World Trade Center). A final photo from the 103rd-floor Skydeck sums it up: an endless, expansive vista of Chicago.

MUST-SNAP SIGHTS BEYOND THE LOOP
> Wrigley Field (p79)
> Pilsen Murals (p128)
> University of Chicago architecture (p143)
> View from the top of the Navy Pier Ferris wheel (p49)
> Dressing up like a hot dog at the Historical Museum (p69)

CHICAGO PHOTOS ON DISPLAY
> City Gallery (p59)
> Photo collection at Chicago Cultural Center (p37)
> Museum of Contemporary Photography (p134)
> Lobby of Second City theater (p77)

Top left The iconic Chicago Theatre (p40) sign **Above** Sears Tower (center; p41): mind-blowing views in both directions

PUBLIC ART

Since a stroll around a few blocks of the Loop is like wandering through a crowded urban sculpture garden – what with works by Picasso, Miró, Chagall and Calder jammed within blocks of each other – there's some irony in the fact that the city's whimsical CowParade, a herd of the-matically painted fiberglass cows on sidewalks around town, was the public-art concept that cities around the world have been inspired to rip off. Chicago's approach to public art is unique in its devotedly earnest, if slightly awkward collision of both high- and lowbrow concepts, faithfully supported by its citizenry since 1978, when the Chicago City Council unanimously approved an ordinance stipulating that a percentage of the cost of constructing or renovating municipal buildings be set aside for commissioning and buying artworks.

Picasso's **Untitled** (Map pp38-9; 50 W Washington St) is the granddaddy of downtown public artworks, looking like it wouldn't mind eating all the cows for breakfast. Other brilliant works in the area include Joan Miró's work **Chicago** (Map pp38-9; 69 W Washington St), originally called *The Sun, The Moon and One Star*; Jean Dubuffet's **Monument with Standing Beast** (Map pp38-9; 100 W Randolph St), nicknamed 'Snoopy in a Blender'; Marc Chagall's **Four Seasons** (Map pp38-9; plaza at Dearborn & Monroe Sts); and Alexander Calder's soaring red sculpture **Flamingo** (Map pp38-9; plaza at Dearborn & Adams Sts). For the locations of more public artworks stashed around the city, pick up a copy of Chicago Public Art Guide at any visitors center, or check the website www.cityofchicago.org/publicart. And don't forget to visit The Bean (see p41), the reigning Loop favorite.

BARS

A signed portrait of Old Blue Eyes – Sinatra himself – beams down over the bar at Gene & Georgetti (p54), an old-world Italian joint where the drink menu bears a simple dedication 'to those merry souls of other days…who, whatever they may drink, prove able to carry it, enjoy it, and remain gentlemen.' By the abundance of taverns in Chicago, it's clear that Chicago's merry souls enjoy a bit of the drink every bit as much as those merry souls. As for the remaining gentlemen? Well, aside from the stumbling coeds in Lincoln Park and the boisterous postgame mobs in Wrigleyville, the city approaches drinking with gentlemanly diligence. Knocking back bottles at a linoleum-floored Ukrainian Village tavern or consulting haute food pairings at a sophisticated speakeasy, Chicago's drinking culture is nothing if not a serious, widely cherished civic pastime.

To really toast Chicago's drinking culture, get the heck out of the Loop and into one of the outlying neighborhoods. There, the proud corner taverns populated by the immigrants who built this city are still marked by a swinging Old Style sign out front. No-nonsense gripes about 'da Mayor' and ice-cold bottles will tell you you've found the right spot.

BEST BAR FOOD
> Hopleaf (p98)
> Violet Hour (p109)
> Gage (p43)
> Kuma's Corner (p117)
> Piece (p107)

BLOCKS FOR BAR HOPPING
> Clark St in Lake View (Map pp80–1, E4)
> Division St in Ukrainian Village (Map pp102–3, C5)
> Lincoln Ave in Lincoln Park (Map pp70–1, D2)
> Damen Ave in Bucktown (Map pp102–3, D2)
> Milwaukee Ave in Wicker Park (Map pp102–3, D3)

BEST COCKTAILS
> Violet Hour (p109)
> Matchbox (p109)
> Gibson's (p65)
> Delilah's (p75)

BEST NEIGHBORHOOD BARS
> Danny's (p108)
> Sterch's (p76)
> Olde Town Ale House (p75)
> Happy Village (p108)
> Charleston (p108)

CYCLING CHICAGO

Jumping in the saddle and cruising the 18.5-mile Lakefront Path is an ideal way to spend a breezy afternoon in Chicago, but since the city is pancake flat and lined with bike lanes everywhere, cycling is also an excellent way to get around if you're willing to strap on a helmet and brave the traffic. The city's **Department of Transportation** (www.chicagobikes.org) offers a free map of bike-friendly streets, plus info on bike shops, publications, local regulations and plenty of other resources. The **Chicagoland Bicycle Federation** (www.biketraffic.org) advocates to make the city even more bike friendly, hosting a website with events and more resources. Chicago offers a great gift to bikers in the form of the **McDonald's Cycle Center** (www.chicagobikestation.com) at Millennium Park, where you can get rentals (per hour/day $8/34), including tandem and children's bikes. **Bike Chicago** (www.bikechicago.com), the rental company here, has outlets on Navy Pier and North Ave Beach and offers free guided bike tours three times a day (at 10am, 1pm and 6:30pm).

To ride a bit longer, consider buying a recycled steed from Working Bikes Cooperative (p129), where sturdy, well-oiled machines begin at about $40 and proceeds go to sending bikes to developing countries. If you're keen to go on a group ride, try **Critical Mass** (www.chicagocriticalmass.org), which takes over the streets starting from Daley Plaza (on the corner of Dearborn and Washington Sts; Map pp38–9, D3) on the last Friday of the month at 5:30pm, or the wonderful **Bike the Drive** (www.bikethedrive.org) on the Memorial Day weekend.

MAJOR THROUGHWAYS FOR BICYCLES

> Halsted St – from Chinatown to Wrigleyville
> Milwaukee Ave – from Near North to Logan Sq
> Lincoln Ave – from Lake View to Old Town
> Roosevelt Rd – from the South Loop to Pilsen
> Damen Ave – from Near West Side to Bucktown

BEST BIKE RIDES

> Lakefront Path (Map pp38–9, start H1, end H5)
> Lincoln Park (Map pp70–1, G3)
> Bike the Drive (Map pp38–9, start G4, end H1)
> Oak St Beach (Map pp60–1, start G3, end G1)
> North Ave Beach to Navy Pier (Map pp50–1, start E3, end H4)

MUSEUMS

Dress up like a human-sized hot dog, navigate a German U-boat and go nose-to-nose with a hammerhead shark. In Chicago's encrusted crown of attractions, the brightest jewels might be the city's collection of world-class museums, many of which are clustered in the Loop and South Loop.

Now for some advice: pick your target wisely and don't try to rush your way through. Any one of the major museums would require a full two-day visit to explore thoroughly, especially larger institutions such as the Field Museum (pictured below) and the Art Institute of Chicago. That said, if you want the city's excellent museums to be a major part of your visit, look into buying a three-, five- or seven-day **Go Chicago Card** (www.gochicagocard.com), which will give you access to a slew of major sites – including museums, zoos, Navy Pier attractions and the Sears Tower Skydeck – and let you return multiple times for one price. If you're concerned that younger traveling companions will be bored stiff, you shouldn't be: in the last couple of decades, most of the museums have refined their experiences for kids into thrilling hands-on multimedia extravaganzas, making the city's museum offerings for children unparalleled.

BEST EXHIBITS
> Sue, the Field Museum (p131)
> U-505 submarine, Museum of Science & Industry (p142)
> Impressionist and American collections, Art Institute of Chicago (p37)
> Regenstein African Journey, Lincoln Park Zoo (p69)

MUST-SEE MUSEUMS
> Chicago History Museum (p69)
> Art Institute of Chicago (p37)
> Field Museum (p131)
> Museum of Contemporary Art (p59)
> Shedd Aquarium (p135)

A DAY AT THE BEACH

After the long, frigid winter, Chicagoans celebrate summer by hitting the miles of sandy beaches on the shores of Lake Michigan to spike volley-balls, splash around or spread a towel and soak up the summer sun. The stampede of joggers signals the start of the waterfront season when the weather starts to break in late April, and by the time the sweltering heat and sticky humidity of August peaks, making the water a dreamy 70°F (21°C), Chicago's shoreline resembles Miami of the Midwest.

In total there are over 30 sandy stretches along Lake Michigan, such as Gillson Park Beach (pictured below), all operated by the **Park District** (☎ 312-742-7529; www.chicagoparkdistrict.com); a trip in the summertime begs digging your toes into the sand of one of them. Lifeguards patrol the shore between May and early September, and though the beaches all attract swimmers, some have special draws. The North Ave Beach, for instance, has the vibe of a Beach Boys song, as the tanned and lovely take turns applying lotion on each other. The 12th St Beach (p138), on the other hand, is a quieter scene, a secluded waterfront retreat hidden near Museum Campus.

RESOURCES TO GET OUT ON THE WATER

> Chicago Kitesurfing (www.chicago kitesurfing.com)
> Chicago Kayak (www.kayakchicago .com)
> Chicago River Canoe & Kayak (www .chicagoriverpaddle.com)
> Wateriders (www.wateriders.com)

> Chicago Architecture Foundation River Tour (www.architecture.org)

BEST BEACHES

> Fullerton Beach (Map pp70–1, G2)
> Oak St Beach (p67)
> 12th St Beach (p138)
> 57th St Beach (Map p141, E3)
> Jackson Park Beach (Map p141, F4)

PERFORMING ARTS

Although its casual art forms – improv comedy and electric blues (see the boxed text, p139) – bear Chicago's unique civic fingerprints, the city's long custom of traditional performing arts hasn't faltered since the fat-cat industrialists developed world-class institutions of high culture. The city supports *two* professional ballet companies (Joffrey Ballet, p47, and Ballet Chicago), a venerated Civic Opera (see p47) and the Chicago Symphony (p45), which is constantly among the finest American orchestras. This is the city that invented jazz dance, and modern companies, such as Hubbard Street Dance (p45), artfully push the form.

The quality theater palaces of the Loop – Auditorium Theater (Map pp38–9, E5), Cadillac Palace Theater (Map pp38–9, C2), Chicago Theatre (p40), Ford Center/Oriental Theater (Map pp38–9, D2) and LaSalle Bank Theatre (Map pp38–9, D3) – serve as pre-Broadway proving grounds for major productions, while the city's venerated dramatic houses, such as Lincoln Park's landmark stage, Steppenwolf, or the Looking Glass Theater, offer season after season of groundbreaking programming. Of course, the fringes offer just as much action through small performance spaces such as Elastic Arts Foundation (p118). Check listings in the *Reader* and *Time Out* to help guide you toward the right rising curtain.

CHICAGO'S HIPPEST PERFORMING-ARTS SPACES
> Elastic Arts Foundation (p118)
> Hubbard St Dance (p45)
> Redmoon Theater (p111)
> Steppenwolf Theater (p77)

BEST CHICAGO DRAMA HOUSES
> Goodman Theater (p45)
> Looking Glass Theater (p59)
> Steppenwolf Theater (p77; pictured above)
> Black Ensemble Theater (p98)

SNAPSHOTS

CHICAGO WITH KIDS

If you plan your trip right, you might think Chicago was built on the colossal scale of a child's imagination – from the hands-on art and educational exhibits within the city's hallowed museums (the Art Institute's touch gallery is particularly riveting) to the Chicago Children's Museum (p56), built with the express purpose of blowing developing minds. Located within Navy Pier, the many kid delights at the Children's Museum include a three-story schooner, a splash park and a hands-on dinosaur dig. All year long families gravitate toward the surrounding Navy Pier, a haven of junk food, carnival rides (pictured below) and fireworks that's the city's most popular tourist destination. For a more offbeat afternoon, parents might want to try the city's inimitable public access indie rock dance party for kids, **Chic-A-Go-Go** (www.roctober.com/chicagogo; #617, 1507 E 53rd St), hosted by the chipper Miss Mia and her little buddy Ratso, a puppet. The illustrious list of the show's alumni includes The Sea and Cake, Sleater-Kinney and TV on the Radio.

Many of the city's best experiences for children are free. In summer, take the kids to one of Lake Michigan's sandy beaches (the Oak St Beach is the most family friendly) or splash around with the squealing mob of youngsters at Millennium Park's *Crown Fountain*. The Lincoln Park Zoo is one of Chicago's great freebies for families.

OUTDOOR FUN FOR KIDS
> Oak St Beach (p67)
> Crown Fountain, in Millennium Park (p41)
> Lincoln Park Zoo (p69)
> Navy Pier Ferris wheel (p49)
> Bike Chicago Millennium Park (p45)

BEST MUSEUM PROGRAMS FOR KIDS
> Chicago Children's Museum (p56)
> Art Institute of Chicago (p37)
> Shedd Aquarium (p135)
> Museum of Science & Industry (p142)
> Visiting Sue at the Field Museum (p131)

CLUBBING & NIGHTLIFE

You might say that the modern concept of clubbing was born right here. In the early '80s at a now-defunct West Side nightclub called the Warehouse, DJ Frankie Knuckles burned out on spinning disco and mashed up European electronic music and beats from this new-fangled invention, the drum machine. In a thump, house music was born. But Chicago's club scene is no longer the glow-stick-and-pill-popping paradise of yore; it has grown up a lot in the last decade, offering a huge breadth of experiences, from the cavernous mega-clubs where pretty people skirt beyond the velvet rope, to tiny spots where people come to get seriously sweaty and hold DJs to a high standard.

If you're into live music, choosing a place to catch some tunes in the city will reveal that Chicago has a burden of riches when it comes to high-quality live-music venues, from intimate little indie rock venues such as the Hideout (p110) and Schubas (p91), to crooner piano bars like Coq d'Or (p66).

BEST LOW-KEY PLACES TO HEAR LOCAL TALENT
> Schubas (p91)
> Hideout (p110)
> Empty Bottle (p110)
> Hungry Brain (p89)
> Charleston (p108)

DANCE CLUBS
> Crobar (p76)
> Le Passage (p66)
> Enclave (p66)
> Leg Room (p67)

SNAPSHOTS

GALLERY DISTRICTS

Sure, 'American Gothic' and the warhorses at the Art Institute are nice for a peek, but what if you want to take some art home with you? Chicago has three gallery-rich neighborhoods, all relatively near the center of town. The most established of these, the River North Gallery District (Map pp50–1, A2) is the most illustrious, with art from top international names and price tags to match. This district is also quite tidy, bordered by Wells, Orleans, Chicago and Erie Sts. It claims to be the largest concentration of private galleries in the United States outside Manhattan. Most are very welcoming and the neighborhood frequently opens its doors for a festive, wine-addled art hop. High rent has moved some of the galleries in this area to cheaper digs in the West Loop or Pilsen.

Speaking of the West Loop and Pilsen… The former brings Chicago's edgier works of younger artists, including many painters, photographers and adventurous mixed-media artists of modest renown. Getting that special something to tie the room together still won't be cheap – anywhere from $500 to $5000 – but most of the galleries are a bit more exciting than their vetted neighbors on the other side of the river. Pilsen is the youngest and most casual art district in town; work here is largely by Chicago locals and there is a good deal of folk art.

CHICAGO ART ON THE WEB
> Chicago Art Dealers Association (www.chicagoartdealers.org)
> Chicago Gallery News (www.chicago gallerynews.com)
> Chicago Artists Coalition (www .caconline.org)
> Art Chicago Festival (www.artchicago .com)

BEST PLACES TO REFUEL AFTER THE GALLERY CRAWL
> Nuevo Leon (p127), Pilsen Gallery District
> Frontera Grill (p54), River North Gallery District
> Gene & Georgetti (p54), River North Gallery District
> Avec (p126), West Loop Gallery District

SPORTS

When it comes to legends of Chicago sport – names such as Jordan, Ditka, Piniella and Chelios – the athletes who represent this city are little short of cultural heroes and the teams for whom they play are cheered, mourned and berated by fierce fans.

Chicago is one of the few cities in the United States with two professional baseball teams – the White Sox and the Cubs – and their allegiance is a litmus test for fans. The Cubs are the lovable losers on the North Side who attract record-breaking numbers of yuppies despite predictably miserable disappointments. The White Sox are the working man's team on the 'Sout Side,' more successful, if less venerated.

Behind the boys of summer, most other franchises take something of a back seat. The Bulls, still fervently followed and well attended, have never recaptured the glory of their mid-'90s rein under Michael Jordan. The Bears, once one of the most revered team of bruisers in the NFL, slumped miserably for the better part of the decade, only to surprise everyone with a trip to the Super Bowl in 2007. They lost the game, and are still regrouping

Which leaves the Blackhawks, the runt of the bunch. The 'Hawks' haven't taken home a Stanley Cup since 1961 and are the neglected child in town. However, the fervor does pick up when rivals such as the Detroit Red Wings or the New York Rangers skate into the United Center (p129), which the Blackhawks share with the Bulls.

TOP CHICAGO SPORTS BLOGS

> Bleed Cubbie Blue (www.bleedcub bieblue.com)
> South Side Sox (www.southsidesox .com)
> Da Bears Blog (www.dabearsblog .com)
> Blog-A-Bull (www.blogabull.com)

WRIGLEYVILLE ON GAME DAY

> Make custom Cubs shirt at Strange Cargo (p83)
> Have a beer at Murphy's Bleachers (p89)
> If you can't score tickets, check out the view from the 'knothole' (p79)
> Party at Yak-Zies (p89)
> Soak up the beers at Clark Street Dog (p84)

LITERARY CHICAGO

The guidebook that you're holding in your hands has insight about where to eat and drink and play in Chicago, but if you want a guidebook to Chicago's soul, look no further than Nelson Algren's *Chicago: City on the Make*. Algren, one of Chicago's literary illuminati, writes of a city that 'forever keeps two faces, one for winners and one for losers; one for hustlers and one for squares… One for early risers, one for evening hiders. One for the White Sox and one for the Cubs.' Today Chicago's literary world still has two faces – one for the postured institutional publications such as *Poetry* and another for literary magazines like *Other Voices*.

Algren captures this dichotomy perfectly: 'Like loving a woman with a broken nose, you may well find lovelier lovelies. But never a lovely so real.'

In the past few years, that woman with a broken nose has been kind to the literary aspirants, and although Chicago is still outshined by lovelier lovelies in the US, the activity within the community has dramatically flourished.

The annual **Chicago Humanities Festival** (www.chfestival.org) makes the end of October a great time of year for visiting book-lovers; the **Printers' Ball** (www.printersball.org), held in the summer, is a bit more of an underground affair. To get a feel for Chicago letters year-round, pick up a copy of *Make* (www.makemag.com) and *ACM*, the full self-effacing title of which, Another Chicago Magazine, perfectly exemplifies the literary scene's underdog spirit.

SEMINAL CHICAGO FICTION

> *The Jungle* (1906, Upton Sinclair)
> *The Man with the Golden Arm* (1949, Nelson Algren)
> *The Adventures of Augie March* (1953, Saul Bellow)
> *Windy City Blues* (1996, Sara Paretsky)
> *The Devil in the White City* (2004, Eric Larson)

BOOKWORM BY DAY, SECRET AGENT BY NIGHT

> 57th Street Books (p144)
> Myopic Books (p104)
> Prairie Avenue Bookshop (p43)
> Women & Children First (p95)
> Boring Store (p101)

Top left 57th Street Books (p144): for serious literary fiends **Above** A bastion of underground culture at Quimby's (p104)

SNAPSHOTS

COMEDY

The kings and queens of the Second City (p77; pictured below) – names such as Aykroyd, Farley, Poehler and Fey among them – rank among some of the greatest comedic minds in modern America, earning Chicago's reputation for bleeding-edge comedy one guffaw at a time. An evening in Second City's Old Town headquarters is one of the banner entertainment opportunities offered by a trip to Chicago.

In no small part because of the influence of Second City, an evening of humor in Chicago is much more likely to come from improv and sketch comedy than stand-up. Chicago's famous comedic names and ensembles descend on stages around the city for the **Chicago Improv Festival** (☎ 773-935-9810; www.chicagoimprovfestival.org) every spring. Recently the festival has included a College Improv Tournament, which draws from a national pool of aspiring coeds who face off in a tournament bracket. Year-round, you'll find laughs at other stages around town, especially in Wrigleyville, home to the IO (ImprovOlympic; p90), which is credited with creating the long-form improv skits, and the rapid-fire Neo-Futurists (p99), whose long-running *Too Much Light Makes the Baby Go Blind: 30 Plays in 60 Minutes* will leave you breathless.

A NIGHT AT THE IMPROV
> Second City (p77)
> IO (ImprovOlympic; p90)
> Comedy Sportz (p90)
> Neo-Futurists (p99)

ALUMNI OF CHICAGO COMEDY
> John Belushi
> Chris Farley
> Bill Murray
> Tina Fey
> Amy Sedaris

The exquisite beaux arts Chicago Cultural Center (p37), the Loop

BACKGROUND

HISTORY

The stories that make up Chicago's historical narrative are both stunningly innovative and savagely brutal, as much about the hope and courage of immigrants who arrived to work in factories and stockyards, as they are about the predatory power brokers who took them for all they were worth. They are about a gangster, Capone, and a statesman, Obama. They revolve around an architect, Burnham, a farmer, Mrs O'Leary, and a pair of Daley mayors. Chicago's stories are written with creativity, and cruelty, in the blood of laborers, the batons of cops and the brilliance of a skyline that continues to reach higher into the heavens.

UP FROM THE ONION PATCH

Like all major American cities, the patch of land that became Chicago was once the turf of Native Americans – the Potawatomi tribe held it last – and they named the area around the mouth of the Chicago River 'Checaugou' (Wild Onions). In the late 1770s the first outsider showed up, Jean Baptiste Pointe Du Sable, the son of a Haitian slave and a French pirate. He married a Potawatomi woman and started trading furs and grain near the spot where the Michigan Ave bridge now stands. In the lead-up to the War of 1812 between the US and Britain, American troops erected Fort Dearborn near Du Sable's original site, but military presence didn't jive with the Potawatomi, who killed 52 fleeing settlers in what's remembered as either the 'Battle' or 'Massacre' of Fort Dearborn – depending on where your sympathies lie.

When the war ended, Chicago grew with frightful speed. The fertile Illinois soil supported farmers, and soon the Illinois & Michigan Canal – a state project linking the Great Lakes to the Illinois River, and thus to the Mississippi River and Atlantic coast – was used to ship grain to cities in the east, establishing Chicago as a transportation hub. It was founded as a town in 1833, with a population of 340 and teeming with 20,000 in a decade.

Railroad tracks soon radiated from the city, as it served as the chugging heart for America's freight and passenger trains. By the end of the 1850s, the railroad and grain trade was making people rich, and the population topped 100,000.

In a harbinger of the city's conventioneering future, the Republican Party hosted its national convention here in 1860, selecting Abraham

Lincoln as its presidential candidate. Like many northern industrial cities, Chicago profited from the Civil War, which drove steel and tool-making industries. But it wasn't until1865, the year the war ended, that the city met its meaty date with destiny: the Union Stockyards opened on the South Side. With new industry came increased demands for workers' rights, and the fight for the right to an eight-hour workday and decent pay set off the riots in Haymarket Sq in 1886, birthing the modern labor movement. Between 1870 and 1900 these myriad industries helped Chicago swell to nearly 1.7 million, the fastest-growing city ever at the time.

UP FROM THE ASHES

But oh, the growing pains!

First it was the nasty water: stockyard effluvia polluted the Chicago River and Lake Michigan and thousands died of cholera and other epidemics. Engineers eventually had to deepen the canal to make the Chicago River flow south, which flushed away city waste to the stinking chagrin of the downstate residents.

Then, the fire: on October 8, 1871, a blaze started southwest of downtown. It burned for three days, killed 300 people, destroyed 18,000 buildings and left 90,000 homeless. The event was wrongfully blamed on Mrs O'Leary's lantern-kicking cow, though the beast was later exonerated by the city council and memorialized by the CowParade (see p158).

There was one silver lining to the disaster: a thriving city with loads of space and money to start from scratch, and ideal conditions for aspiring architects in the 1880s and '90s. Daniel Burnham was one of the premier designers and his bold, artful urban footprint included green space and public art. He summed up the city's credo best: 'Make no little plans,' he counseled Chicago's leaders in 1909, 'for they have no magic to stir men's blood… Make big plans.' The big plans yielded big buildings; the world's first skyscraper was built here in 1885 (for more on architecture, see p150).

There was no lack of magic when Burnham and other visionaries built the complex of the 1893 World's Columbian Exposition, Chicago's flamboyant debut on the international stage. The semidisposable structures by Hyde Park were gleaming white and brilliantly lit, a pristine experiment in harmonious urban planning. Many of the 27 million visitors rode the new El train to the fair, marveling at long-distance phone calls, moving pictures and the Ferris wheel. This was also when Pabst beer won the blue ribbon that has been part of its name ever since.

THE GREAT MIGRATION & GANGSTERS

Almost two decades after the 'White City' was dismantled, Chicago's population saw a huge influx of Southern blacks, in what came to be known as the 'Great Migration,' as people fled the fractured states of the Confederacy. Chicago employers promised jobs to anyone willing to work, and the migrants, often poorly educated sharecroppers with big dreams, poured into the city. When these workers arrived, things weren't so rosy though. Factory bosses broke white unions and hired cheaper, nonunionized labor in the form of the new Chicagoans, resulting in a steep rise in racial tension. In 1919 the city's first race riots killed 38 residents, black and white.

There was more civil unrest the next year, when the nationwide enactment of Prohibition – a federal constitutional amendment prohibiting alcohol consumption – made Chicago dry, even after voters had gone six to one against the law in an advisory referendum. The city's efforts to flout Prohibition gave rise to Al Capone, whose notorious bootlegging and organized crime syndicate captured the American imagination.

For years Chicago was synonymous with Capone, a ruthless, wry-witted prototype of the Italian-American gangster. Between 1924 and 1931 (when he was busted for taxes) he got rich off Chicago's thirst for booze, expanding his entrepreneurial interests to include gambling and prostitution, and pulling off brazen, bloody assaults on his enemies, such as the St Valentine's Day Massacre.

WELCOME TO THE MACHINE

When Prohibition was repealed in 1933, the city hosted another World's Fair and Ed Kelly became mayor, rolling out Democratic 'machine politics.' Politicians gave city jobs and lucrative contracts to people who worked hard to get him elected. It was a pretty simple machine.

The zenith of the machine's power began with the election of Richard J Daley ('the Boss') in 1955. He ran the machine with ease, dispatching enemies and winning five times in a row before dying in office in 1976.

Although the machine was a forceful political mechanism that modernized the city, the shortcomings of Daley's political style were never more clearly displayed than in 1968, a year that proved volatile for Chicago. First, the assassination of Martin Luther King Jr in Memphis set off unstoppable riots on Chicago's West Side. Later, when Chicago hosted the Democratic National Convention, Daly's reaction to anti-Vietnam war demonstrators turned the city into a police state resulting in savage, televised beatings.

HISTORIC SITES

> Water Tower (p59)
> St Valentine's Day Massacre Site (Map pp70–1)
> Haymarket Sq (p122)
> Site of the first controlled nuclear reaction (University of Chicago, p143)

The long-term effects of the riots were huge. The Democratic candidate for president, Hubert Humphrey, was left without liberal backing after his support of Daley helped Richard Nixon win the presidency. As if Chicago's reputation could get worse, the financial pressures of the early '70s closed the last of the stockyards and the city's manufacturing sector headed for the 'burbs or the southern states, where taxes and wages were lower.

Just as it was looking like Chicago's sad economic fate would be akin to 'Rust Belt' northern neighbors such as Detroit and Cleveland, the Sears Tower opened in 1974, beginning a development trend in the Loop that brought in thousands of high-paying white-collar jobs. In 1975 the Water Tower Place mall brought new life to N Michigan Ave, signaling the first steps of the Magnificent Mile.

CHICAGO TODAY

Today you might still hear talk of the 'Second City' – a disparaging nickname given from a 1952 *New Yorker* article – but Chicago is taking a backseat to no one. It just delivered a historic president and was the only US city shortlisted for the 2016 Olympic Games.

Much has to do with the man in the mayor's chair, the Boss' son, Richard M Daley, whose civic projects, such as Millennium Park and an immaculate downtown, have delivered Chicago to the center of the world's stage. But much of it also has to do with the crackling optimism that's tangible in the streets. Chicago is a city whose moment in history has arrived.

LIFE AS A CHICAGO RESIDENT

If you were to paint a picture of a Chicago resident using only the statistics, you'd see a person spending their early 30s living in the third-biggest city in the United States, most likely a white Democrat with some college education or a bachelor's degree. They'd commute more than 25 minutes every day to a job in the technology or air-travel sector, where they'd make about $38,000 a year. But if this vanilla picture is discordant with what you see when you visit, it's because Chicago is a city of great racial, economic and cultural diversity, mixed in largely equal measure.

Latinos make up around 20% of the city's population, and so do blacks. The city's growing Asian population is currently around 5%.

Chicago is a fairly young city, with a median age of 32, lower than the national average by four years, but residents have to stop eating hot dogs and knocking back Old Style – Chicago spends a greater amount on food than the national average and is regularly one of America's fattest cities.

Popular Science magazine recently ranked Chicago as one of the greenest cities in America, helped by 12,000 acres of open space and new investments in recycling and tree planting. Daley's pet project to plant carbon-sequestering vegetation on over 4.5 million sq ft of rooftops has also given the city a reputation for a progressive stance on carbon emissions.

Financially, Chicago is fairly flush. Most of the workforce heads to a white-collar job, even though the city leads the nation in manufacturing. But the city today is made up of the same stark dichotomies as it always has: Chicago's cost of living is 26.45% higher than the US average, but 20% of its residents live below the poverty line, mostly on Chicago's sprawling South Side. Those ghettos are kept far from the tourist brochures, and they stand in harsh contrast to the mansions of the Gold Coast.

The residents put up with a fairly harsh winter – January high temperatures aren't above freezing and it averages about a foot of snow – so when summer comes, with 84°F temperatures in July, residents make the most of it, flocking to the shore of Lake Michigan and attending a constantly booked festival calendar (see p21).

WINDY CITY INVENTIONS

> Roller skates (1884)
> Hostess Twinkies (1930)
> Pinball (1930)
> Controlled atomic reaction (1942)
> Daytime TV soap operas (1949)
> Spray paint (1949)
> Lava Lite 'Lava Lamps' (1965)
> House music (1977)

GOVERNMENT & POLITICS

It's unknown who was the first Chicagoan to advise the citizenry to 'vote early and often' but most people think it was either legendary gang boss Al Capone or William 'Big Bill' Thompson, a mayor who once held a debate between himself and two live rats (to represent his opponents, naturally). Regardless, the four words speak volumes about the somewhat checkered reputation of Chicago's political culture.

But that reputation has changed a lot in recent years, mostly because of a former South Side community organizer and University of Chicago professor who became the first black president: Barack Obama. Chicago is still basking in Obama's dizzying political ascent, and the glory is not likely to fade any time soon. In many ways Obama shaped his political disposition after his idol, Illinois' *other* groundbreaking president, Abraham Lincoln.

As you zoom in a bit from Chicago's plays on the national political stage, things get a little less rosy. First, there's recently impeached Illinois governor Rod Blagojevich, who was issued out of office for trying to sell Obama's vacant senate seat to the highest bidder. 'Blago' was a replacement for George Ryan, another former governor who was convicted on federal racketeering charges. Then there's Chicago's infatuation with the Daley mayoral rein, which stretches back generations.

The current mayor, Richard M Daley, is the son of Richard J Daley, who held the office for years. Both Daleys have navigated their post with shrewd political instincts, helping to win state and federal money for huge infrastructure projects, such as an O'Hare airport expansion, a huge addition to the McCormick Place Convention Center and the reconstruction of Navy Pier. Richard M Daley has a penchant for colorful banter with the press, such as this classic explanation for why city health inspectors had closed down so many local restaurants: 'Whadda ya want? A rat in yer sandwich or a mouse in yer salad?'

Maybe the most notable of the Daleys' similarities, however, is their ability to hold on to their job. Richard M Daley won his re-election bids from 1991 to 2007, pretty much by a landslide every time. If he finishes out his current term through 2010, he'll become Chicago's longest-running mayor. The previous record holder? His dad, who was Chicago's mayor for 21 years.

Daley leads a council of 50 alderman and, given the size of the body and the occasionally contentious infighting, observing the city's politics remains a beloved and bemoaned civic pastime.

FURTHER READING
NONFICTION
The Devil in the White City (2004, Eric Larson) A gripping bit of nonfiction about the World's Co-lumbian Exposition, which was held in Chicago in 1893 and inadvertently became the playground of one of America's first serial killers.

Dreams from My Father: A Story of Race and Inheritance (2006, Barack Obama) Obama's first book chronicles his search for racial identity and his rise in Chicago politics.

Murder City: The Bloody History of Chicago in the Twenties (2007, Michael Lesy) Blood pours out of these pages that chronicle Chicago in the 1920s, when it was America's murder capital.

One More Time: The Best of Mike Royko (1999, Mike Royko) Royko's view on dirty politics and daily life in Chicago at the now-defunct *Daily News* won him a Pulitzer in 1972. These earnest, snappy, often poignant vignettes of Chicago add up to a rollercoaster read.

Working: People Talk About What They Do All Day and How They Feel About What They Do (1974, Studs Turkel) This exploration into the meaning of work from people in all walks of life is a seminal text for 'the city that works.'

FICTION
The Adventures of Augie March (1953, Saul Bellow) Often listed among the best American novels, this celebrated father of Chicago fiction paints an engaging portrayal of a destitute boy's experiences during the Depression.

The House on Mango Street (1984, Sandra Cisneros) This collection of interconnected vignettes is set in a Mexican-American Chicago barrio.

I Sailed with Magellan (2004, Stuart Dybek) First recognized for 1990's *The Coast of Chicago*, Dybek's second major collection of stories is an impressive update of the down-and-out narratives of Nelson Algren.

The Jungle (1906, Upton Sinclair) This epic from 1906 is set on the brutal, blood-soaked floors of Chicago's South Side meatpacking plants. It cast a bright light on the inhumane working conditions of Chicago's immigrant communities and was a catalyst for reform.

The Man with the Golden Arm (1949, Nelson Algren) A tale of a drug-addicted kid on Division St, this won the National Book Award in 1950. These days a walk down the same stretch of Division is more likely to get you addicted to clothes from Urban Outfitters.

POETRY
Annie Allen (1949, Gwendolyn Brooks) This collection of poems made Brooks the first African American writer ever to receive a Pulitzer Prize.

The City in Which I Love You (1990, Li-Young Lee) The composed verse of this contemporary Asian American voice evokes traditional Chinese poets such as Li Bo.

DIRECTORY
TRANSPORTATION
ARRIVAL & DEPARTURE
AIR

O'Hare is a bit bigger and slightly further away from downtown, but both it and Midway are well connected to the city center. O'Hare lies about 17 miles to the northwest of the Loop, right off the I-90, and Midway lies about 10 miles southwest, off I-55. Both airports have police stations, ATMs and pay phones (some TTY capable). Wireless internet is available for $6.95 per day. For shuttle rides between Midway and O'Hare airports, use the **Omega Shuttle** (☎ 773-483-6634; www.omegashuttle.com; per person $16).

O'Hare International Airport

O'Hare (ORD; ☎ 773-686-2200; www .ohare.com) is the nation's second-busiest airport, hopping day and night. If you pass through here, you'll be one of 80 million passengers it hosts every year. United Airlines has its headquarters here, and it is one of many carriers that uses the hub. O'Hare has every amenity that you might expect from a major American airport. **Visitor information** (⏰ 9am-5pm) is located on the lower level of all terminals. If you're lucky, you'll travel through the Terminal 1 building, designed by architect Helmut Jahn, to Terminal 2 to experience a psychedelic neon-and-colored-glass moving-sidewalk ride, a trippy way to start your visit.

Midway Airport

The tidy little sister of O'Hare, **Midway** (MDW; ☎ 773-838-3003; www.fly chicago.com) was redeveloped in the early 2000s and is smaller and a bit less dog-eared than O'Hare. It's also slightly closer to downtown and equally as accessible to the El train. Most services are located

---

CLIMATE CHANGE & TRAVEL

Travel – especially air travel – is a significant contributor to global climate change. At Lonely Planet, we believe that all who travel have a responsibility to limit their personal impact. As a result, we have teamed with Rough Guides and other concerned industry partners to support Climate Care, which allows people to offset the greenhouse gases they are responsible for with contributions to energy-saving projects and other climate-friendly initiatives in the developing world. Lonely Planet offsets all staff and author travel.

For more information, turn to the responsible travel pages on www.lonelyplanet .com. For details on offsetting your carbon emissions and a carbon calculator, go to www .climatecare.org.

Travel to/from the Airport

	Taxi from O'Hare	Train from O'Hare
Pick-up point	Outside each terminal's arrival area	CTA Blue Line located in terminal 1, 2 and 3 arrival areas, on lowest level of the Parking Garage in the main terminal area
Drop-off point	Anywhere	Downtown stations include Washington, Monroe, Jackson and La Salle
Duration	About 45min to the Loop	45min
Cost	$35-45	$2.25
Other	Note that cab meters keep running even when the car is at a standstill in traffic	Trains run 24hr daily, at 10min intervals during the day
Contact	Cabs will wait in queue outside of terminals	☎ 312-836-7000; www.transitchicago.com

in the New Terminal building, and its modern layout makes it easy to navigate.

TRAIN

Metra (☎ 312-322-6777; www.metrarail .com) runs a web of commuter trains to suburbs surrounding Chicago. Some of the Metra lines run frequent schedules seven days a week; others operate only during weekday rush hours. Short trips start at $1.95.

Chicago's **Union Station** (Map pp38-9, A4; 225 S Canal St) is the hub for **Amtrak** (☎ 800-872-7245; www.amtrak .com), which connects to major

US cities. On Amtrak you can go as far as Los Angeles ($140, 43 hours) or as close as Milwaukee ($21, 1½ hours). Booking several weeks in advance will usually save you money. Amtrak is faster than traveling by Greyhound, and much more comfortable.

GETTING AROUND

Locals may gripe about it, but the Chicago Transit Authority (CTA) is an elaborate and reliable network of buses and 'El' trains that is preferable to traveling the city by car. Most places of interest to travelers in the Loop, Near North and Gold

Taxi From Midway	El From Midway
Taxicabs are available on a first-come, first-served basis from the lower-level curb in front of the terminal	CTA Orange Line is located right across Cicero Ave
Victoria coach station	Makes stops through southwest Chicago and the Loop
25min	30min
$25-35	$2.25
Note that cab meters keep running even when the car is at a standstill in traffic	Follows Piccadilly; avoid using in rush hour if you have large suitcases; no service 12:30am to 5:30am
A list of pre-arranged limousine services is provided at the Ground Transportation Information Booth on baggage claim level, near carousel #4 terminals	☎ 312-836-7000; www.transitchicago.com

Coast neighborhoods are within walking distance. In this book the nearest El station is marked after the Ⓜ in each listing. If bus is a better option, the relevant route will be marked by the 🚌 in each listing.

TRAVEL PASSES
You can save with a visitor pass for El trains and city buses operated by the CTA. Passes for one day ($5.75), three days ($14) or seven days ($23) will save you a bundle and are available from vending machines at many stations. The **Currency Exchange** (Map pp50-1, D3;

☎ 312-944-4643; 62 E Chicago Ave; 🕙 24hr) also sells passes (cash only).

The CTA runs a free **trolley** (www .cityofchicago.org/Transportation/trolleys; 🕙 10am-6pm) during summer and the Christmas holidays, connecting major sights, but be warned: when tourists pack into them on a sweltering July day, you may wish you'd paid for public transport.

THE CHICAGO TRANSIT AUTHORITY
All the El trains and local buses are run by the **Chicago Transit Authority** (CTA; ☎ 312-836-7000; www.transitchicago .com). The El system is an efficient

Recommended Transportation Between Key Destinations

	Millennium Park	Magnificent Mile	Wrigley Field
Millennium Park	n/a	walk 20min	walk then CTA Red Line 25min
Magnificent Mile	walk 20min	n/a	CTA Red Line 20min
Wrigley Field	walk then CTA Red Line 25min	CTA Red Line 20min	n/a
Wicker Park	walk then CTA Blue /Brown Line 15min	bus 66 then CTA Blue Line 30min	bus 152 or 50, 40min
Andersonville	walk then CTA Red Line 45min	bus 147 then walk 35min	bus 22, 15min
Old Town	CTA Brown Line 20min	walk 25min	walk 25min

way to get around, though only the Blue Line from O'Hare to the Loop and the Red Line from Howard to 95/Dan Ryan run 24 hours, about every 15 minutes. Bus routes follow major thoroughfares north–south or east–west. Between the two systems, you can get anywhere in the city. Useful maps are available at stations and on the CTA website.

After a recent fare hike, CTA buses cost $2 and the El costs $2.25. The plastic card tickets have a magnetized strip that allows you to add as much credit as you'd like. Fares (and transfers) are deducted automatically when you enter the El system or board the bus.

AIR TRAVEL ALTERNATIVES

Chicago is a historical transportation hub, and highways and rails still whisk in visitors from every point of the compass. Amtrak services some 500 destinations from Union Station, which is in the heart of downtown. Trips to nearby Midwestern cities, such as St Louis or Milwaukee, take only a few hours. The ride between Chicago and New York City is about 20 hours. Reaching the city on bus is also easy, as it is a hub for Greyhound and a handful of regional bus lines, including **megabus** (www.megabus.com). If you are traveling between major cities and book far in advance, megabus is by far the cheapest option: rides start at $1 and get more expensive as the bookings fill the seats. The highway system is straightforward for drivers, though the most scenic way to reach downtown is along State Rd 41, which hugs the edge of Lake Michigan and connects to Lake Shore Dr.

Wicker Park	Andersonville	Old Town
walk then CTA Blue /Brown Line 15min	walk then CTA Red Line 45min	CTA Brown Line 20min
bus 66 then CTA Red Line 30min	bus 147 then walk 35min	bus 151, 15min
bus 152 or 50, 40min	bus 22, 20min	walk 25min
n/a	bus 50, 40min	bus 72, 15min
bus 50, 40min	n/a	bus 22, 35min
bus 72, 15min	bus 22, 35min	n/a

CAR & MOTORCYCLE

Driving in Chicago is no fun. Traffic snarls not only at rush hours, but also just about every hour in between. Especially for short trips in town, use public transportation to spare yourself the headache.

You'll need a credit card to rent a car, and many agencies only rent to those 25 and older. Expect to pay $30 to $45 per day for a compact, with better weekly rates and reduced rates on weekends. Sometimes booking with an online broker, such as Priceline.com, can drive the cost down to $15 per day.

TAXI

In the Loop through Lincoln Park, taxis are plentiful. In other parts of the city, you might have a long wait if you don't call a cab. It costs $2.25 when you get into the cab,

$1.80 for each additional mile and about 40¢ per minute. Drivers expect a 10% to 15% tip. All major companies accept credit cards. To report a taxi incident, take down the driver's name and cab number, and call the **Department of Customer Services Complaint Hotline** (☎ 311).

Reliable companies:
American-United Taxi (☎ 773-248-7600)
Flash Cab (☎ 773-561-1444; www.flashcab .com)
Yellow Cab (☎ 312-829-4222; www.yellow cabchicago.com)

BOATS

Taking a **Shoreline Sightseeing Water Taxi** (☎ 312-222-9328; www.shoreline sightseeing.com; ⏱ 10am-6pm) is a fun alternative to walking or busing between the city's big-ticket sights. The Lake Taxi (Map pp50–1, G4) transports tourists from the southwestern corner of Navy Pier to the front of the South Loop's Shedd Aquarium (one way adult/child $7/4), while the River Taxi (Map pp50–1, F4) connects the Sears Tower with the mouth of the river at Gateway Park, conveniently just west of popular Navy Pier (one way adult/child $6/3). The Commuter Taxi (Map pp50–1, D4) picks up passengers at the north side of the river, just east of the Michigan Ave bridge, and floats along its merry way to the south side of Adams St, at the Sears Tower, and across from Union Station (one way $3).

The **Chicago Water Taxi** (☎ 312-337-1446; www.chicagowatertaxi.com; ☽ 6:30am-7pm) is another service, primarily for commuters. It ferries between the north shore of the river at Michigan Ave (Map pp50–1, D4) and the east river bank north of Madison St (near the Metra Ogilvie Transportation Center). A one-way ride is $2, an all-day pass $4.

PRACTICALITIES
BUSINESS HOURS

Normal business hours follow:
Banks & most businesses 9am-5pm Mon-Fri
Bars & taverns 11am-2am, some bars until 4am or 5am
Restaurants 11am-10pm, with many 24-hour options
Shops 11am-7pm Mon-Sat, noon-6pm Sun

INFORMATION & ORGANIZATIONS

The **Chicago Tourism Center** (☎ 312-744-6630, 877-244-2246; www.choosechicago.com) has in-depth information on visiting the city on its website, including booking information for centrally located hotels. The City of Chicago runs its own excellent resource site at www.explorechicago.org and operates two strategically located **visitors centers** (☽ 8am-7pm Mon-Thu, 8am-6pm Fri, 9am-6pm Sat, 10am-6pm Sun): in the Loop at 77 E Randolph St and on the Magnificent Mile, at 163 E Pearson Ave, where you can get brochures and information.

INTERNET

Though Chicago ranks among the most connected cities in the US, public libraries remain the best bet for free wired internet access, with the Harold Washington Library (p40) topping the options for people staying downtown; get a 'day pass' at the checkout desk. The Chicago Cultural Center (p37) also has it for free. Many bars and restaurants in Lincoln Park, Bucktown and Near North often have free wi-fi as well. For some more detailed internet research about Chicago, try the following websites:
Gaper's Block (www.gapersblock.com) The latest political and cultural happenings in the Windy City.

Green Maps (www.artic.edu/webspaces /greenmap/) Eateries, shops and other businesses that promote sustainable living choices in Chicago.
Hot Rooms (www.hotrooms.com) Chicago-centric hotel room consolidator.
LTH Forum (www.lthforum.com) Chitchat about the restaurant scene from local foodies.

These walking tours are available for free, so load up that iPod and hit the pavement.
Chicago Loop Alliance (www.chicago loopalliance.com) Offers three downloads taking in various downtown sights: Art Loop, Landmark Loop and Theater Loop.
Chicago Office of Tourism (www.down loadchicagotours.com) Check out the Buddy Guy–narrated blues tour.
Illinois Bureau of Tourism (www .onscreenillinois.com) Tour of famous movie sites such as *The Blues Brothers, Ferris Bueller's Day Off* and *The Untouchables*.

MONEY
The US currency is the dollar ($), divided into 100 cents (¢). Coins come in denominations of 1¢ (penny), 5¢ (nickel), 10¢ (dime), 25¢ (quarter), 50¢ (half dollar – rare) and $1 (silver dollar – rare). Notes (bills) come in denominations of $1, $2 (rare), $5, $10, $20, $50 and $100.

For exchange rates, see the inside front cover of this guide. Meals per person per day will run $15 and up, hotel stays $100 and up, and transportation in the city $3 and up. Of course, if you want to spend more, there's lots of opportunity, and if you want to spend less, try looking for some freebies on p31.

NEWSPAPERS & MAGAZINES
Chicago Magazine (www.chicagomag.com) Monthly magazine with articles and culture coverage slanted toward upscale readers.
Chicago Reader (www.chicagoreader .com) Free weekly alternative newspaper with comprehensive arts and entertainment listings; widely available at bookstores, bars and coffee shops.
Chicago Sun-Times (www.suntimes .com) The *Tribune's* daily, tabloid-esque competitor paper.
Chicago Tribune (www.chicagotribune .com) The city's stalwart daily newspaper; its younger, fluffier version is *RedEye*.
Crain's Chicago Business (www.chicago business.com) Weekly publication covering business news.
Time Out Chicago Hip, service-oriented magazine with all-encompassing listings.
Venus Magazine (www.venuszine.com) Arts-oriented quarterly 'zine for women.

TELEPHONE
The only foreign phones that will work in the US (and Canada) are tri-band models operating on GSM 1900 and other frequencies. If you have a GSM tri-band phone, check with your service provider about using it in the US. Make sure to ask if roaming charges apply, as these can be pricy.

COUNTRY & CITY CODES

The US country code is ☎ 1, and area code ☎ 312 serves Chicago's Loop and an area bounded roughly by North Ave to the north, Ashland Ave to the west and 16th St to the south. The rest of the city falls under area code ☎ 773. The northern suburbs use area code ☎ 847, suburbs to the west and south use ☎ 708, and the far west suburbs use ☎ 630.

USEFUL PHONE NUMBERS

Chicago Convention & Tourism Bureau (☎ 312-567-8500)
Chicago Cultural Center Visitor Information Center (☎ 312-346-3278)
Chicago Fine Arts Hotline (☎ 312-346-3278)
Chicago Office of Tourism (☎ 312-744-2400)
City of Chicago travel counselor hotline (☎ 877-224-2246)
International Direct Dial Code (☎ 011)
Local Directory Inquiries (☎ 411)

TIPPING

Bars Tipping a dollar per drink is the norm, though if you order a round for buddies, a $5 tip should suffice.
Hotel Porters $3 to $5
Restaurants 15% to 20%
Taxis 10%
Valet parking $3

TOURIST INFORMATION

The **Chicago Office of Tourism** (☎ 312-744-2400; www.choosechicago.com) is set up in two highly trafficked locations: the Chicago Cultural Center (p37) in the Loop, and the **Chicago Water Works Visitor Center** (Map pp60-1, G6; 163 E Pearson Ave; ☷ 8am-7pm Mon-Thu, 8am-6pm Fri, 9am-6pm Sat, 10am-6pm Sun) on the Mag Mile. Though both have helpful staff and tons of local information, the main office is the one in the Cultural Center, where you can also drop in for free tours led by volunteers. Additional information, eg on hotel bookings, can be had by calling the staffed tourism hotline on ☎ 877-244-2246.

TRAVELERS WITH DISABILITIES

The **Mayor's Office for People with Disabilities** (☎ 312-744-4496) is great for travelers with disabilities, providing a guide to resources. The office shows how committed the city is to providing fully accessible tourism, with a bus fleet that can accommodate wheelchairs. **Pace** (☎ 800-606-1282; www.pacebus.com) runs buses between Chicago's city center and the outer suburbs, with para-transit services throughout the area for travelers with disabilities.

>INDEX

See also separate subindexes for Drink (p189), Eat (p190), Play (p191), See (p191) and Shop (p192).

ⓨ DRINK

000 map pages

🏠 SHOP

000 map pages